GCSE LAW CASEBOOK

GCSE LAW CASEBOOK

David Corns BA, PGCE

and

Eric Boucher LLB, PGCE, MCIBSE

BLACKSTONE
PRESS LIMITED

First published in Great Britain 1989 by Blackstone Press Limited,
9-15 Aldine Street, London W12 8AW. Telephone: 01-740 1173

ISBN: 1 85431 042 9

British Library Cataloguing in Publication Data
A CIP cataloguing record for this book is available from the British Library

Cartoons drawn by Anne Lee

Typeset by Murdoch Evans Partnership, London EC1
Printed in Great Britain by Billing & Sons Ltd, Worcester

CONTENTS

Introduction 7

Case references 9

Law report abbreviations 10

Table of cases (alphabetical) 11

Table of cases (by type of law) 14

The cases 17

Using cases in an examination 123

For Elizabeth and Vivien

INTRODUCTION

A knowledge of relevant cases and how they should be used in answers is essential if a student is to be successful in GCSE Law. Examiners have often commented that many candidates have failed to support their answers by referring to relevant cases and this omission is one of the most common causes of failure to achieve a good grade of pass in the GCSE examination.

This book aims to provide the student with all case requirements by providing in a single, clear and concise text:

(a) details of many of the cases likely to be needed for GCSE, in a 'case a page' format;
(b) a commentary on the legal significance of each case;
(c) comprehensive indexes;
(d) a guide to the way in which cases should be incorporated into answers.

In limiting this case book to 100 cases there must, inevitably, be some omission of cases which could be useful to GCSE students.

A margin for notes to be added by students is provided at the side of each case.

Although primarily intended for GCSE Law students it is hoped that the clarity of the layout and the straightforward approach will appeal to students commencing the subject at other levels, such as BTEC and GCE 'A' level courses.

We should like to record our thanks to Alistair and all at Blackstone Press for their invaluable help.

CASE REFERENCES

For the benefit of students who have access to a law library and who may wish to read fuller accounts of any case in the law reports, a reference is given under the title of each case.

The reference is set out in the standard form:

Year of case Volume number Report abbreviation Page number

Note that the year of the case is always enclosed in either:

square brackets [ ] to indicate that the year is needed to find the report, the volume number not being sufficient,

or

round brackets ( ) to indicate that the year is not needed to find the report, the volume number being sufficient.

Some confusion may be experienced with case titles involving appeals to the House of Lords, as prior to 1974 these case titles were reversed on such an appeal. For example: *Smith* v *Jones* would become *Jones* v *Smith* if Jones took an appeal to the House of Lords.

A list of law report abbreviations used in this casebook will be found on p. 10.

LAW REPORT ABBREVIATIONS

AC	Appeal Cases Reports (House of Lords/Privy Council)
All ER	All England Weekly Reports
All ER Rep	All England Reports (Reprints)
App Cas	Appeal Cases Reports (prior to 1891)
B & Ad	Barnwell and Adolphus Law Reports
Bing	Bingham Law Reports
Bing NC	Bingham, New Cases
Ch D	Chancery Division of the High Court Reports (prior to 1891)
Ch	Chancery Division of the High Court Reports
Co Rep	Sir Edward Coke Reports
CP	Common Pleas Cases
Cr App Rep	Cohen Criminal Appeal Reports
EG	Estates Gazette
ER/ER Rep	The 'English Reports' (collected reprints of private reports)
Ex D	Exchequer Division of the High Court Reports (before abolition)
Fam	Family Division of the High Court Reports
H & C	Hurlstone and Coltman Law Reports
Hob	Hobart Law Reports
KB	King's Bench of the High Court Reports
LR	Law Reports from 1865 (all courts)
QB	Queen's Bench of the High Court Reports
QBD	Queen's Bench of the High Court Reports (prior to 1891)
RTR	Road Traffic Reports
SJ	Solicitors' Journal Reports
WR	Weekly Reporter
WLR	Weekly Law Reports from 1953 (all courts)

TABLE OF CASES

Allcard v Skinner	17
Appleson v Littlewood Ltd	18
Baker v Hopkins Ltd	19, 41
Balfour v Balfour	20
Beard v London General Omnibus Co.	21, 73
Bell v Lever Bros	22
Bernstein, Baron, of Leigh v Skyview & General Ltd	23, 65
Bisset v Wilkinson	24
Bliss v Hall	25
Bolton v Stone	26
Bourhill v Young	27, 66
Byrne v Deane	28
Campbell v Paddington Borough Council	29
Carlill v Carbolic Smoke Ball Co.	30
Cassidy v Daily Mirror Newspapers Ltd	31
Central London Property Trust Ltd v High Trees House Ltd	32
Chaplin v Leslie Frewin (Publishers) Ltd	33
Christie v Davey	34
Collins v Godefroy	36
Condor v The Barron Knights Ltd	37
Cope v Sharpe	38
Couturier v Hastie	39
Cundy v Lindsay	40
Cutler v United Dairies Ltd	41
Davis Contractors Ltd v Fareham Urban District Council	37, 42
De Francesco v Barnum	43, 109
Derry v Peek	44
Dickinson v Dodds	45
Director of Public Prosecutions v Newbury and Jones	46
Donoghue (or M'Alister) v Stevenson	48
Esso Petroleum v Harper's Garages Ltd	49, 80
Felthouse v Bindley	50
Fisher v Bell	51, 86
Fitch v Dewes	52, 80
Foster v Mackinnon	53
Hadley v Baxendale	54, 119
Hall v Brooklands Auto-Racing Club	55
Harris v Nickerson	56
Harvey v Facey	57
Hedley Byrne & Co. Ltd v Heller & Partners Ltd	58
Henthorn v Fraser	59
Household Fire Insurance Co. v Grant	60

Hyde v Hyde	61
Hyde v Wrench	59, 62, 92
Jones, Re	63
K (Deceased), Re	64
Kelsen v Imperial Tobacco Co.	65
King v Phillips	66
Krell v Henry	67
Lampleigh v Braithwait	68, 73
Leaf v International Galleries	69
Lewis v Averay	71
Limpus v London General Omnibus Co	72
McArdle, Re	73
McLoughlin v O'Brian	27, 74
Mahon v Osborne	75
Merritt v Merritt	76
Nash v Inman	32, 77, 109
National Coal Board v Evans & Co. and another	78
Nichols v Marsland	79
Nordenfelt v Maxim Nordenfelt Guns & Ammunition Co.	80
O'Connor v Swan & Edgar and Carmichael	81
Paris v Stepney Borough Council	82
Parkinson v College of Ambulance Ltd and Harrison	83
Pearce v Brooks	84
Pepper v Webb	85
Pharmaceutical Society of Great Britain v Boots Cash Chemists (Southern) Ltd	86
Phillips v Brooks	87
Phipps v Rochester Corporation	88
Pinnel's Case	89
Planché v Colburn	90
Raffles v Wichelhaus	91
Ramsgate Victoria Hotel Co v Montefiore	92
R v Allen	93
R v Bowsher	94
R v Byrne	95
R v Church	96
R v Collins	98
R v Deller	99
R v Dudley and Stephens	100
R v Halliday	101
R v Lloyd, Bhuee and Ali	102
R v Miller	103
R v Morris	104
R v Nedrick	105

R v Quick	106
R v Tolson	107
Roberts v Gray	33, 109
Robinson v Kilvert	110
Sayers v Harlow Urban District Council	111
Simpkins v Pays	20, 113
Stilk v Myrick	114
Storey v Ashton	21, 115
Sweet v Parsley	116
Taylor v Caldwell	117
Thomas v Thomas	118
Victoria Laundry (Windsor) Ltd v Newman Industries Ltd	54, 119
Wagon Mound, The; Overseas Tankship (UK) Ltd v Morts Dock & Engineering Co.	120
Warner Bros Pictures v Nelson	121
Welch v Cheesman	122

TABLE OF CASES BY TYPE OF LAW

LAW OF CONTRACT

Allcard v Skinner 17
Appleson v Littlewood Ltd 18
Balfour v Balfour 20
Bell v Lever Bros 22
Bisset v Wilkinson 24
Carlill v Carbolic Smoke Ball Co. 30
Central London Property Trust Ltd v High Trees House Ltd 32
Chaplin v Leslie Frewin (Publishers) Ltd 33
Collins v Godefroy 36
Condor v The Barron Knights Ltd 37
Couturier v Hastie 39
Cundy v Lindsay 40
Davis Contractors Ltd v Fareham Urban District Council 42
De Francesco v Barnum 43
Derry v Peek 44
Dickinson v Dodds 45
Esso Petroleum v Harper's Garages Ltd 49
Felthouse v Bindley 50
Fisher v Bell 51
Fitch v Dewes 52
Foster v Mackinnon 53
Hadley v Baxendale 54
Harris v Nickerson 56
Harvey v Facey 57
Hedley Byrne & Co. Ltd v Heller & Partners Ltd 58
Henthorn v Fraser 59
Household Fire Insurance Co. v Grant 60
Hyde v Wrench 62
Krell v Henry 67
Leaf v International Galleries 69
Lewis v Averay 71
McArdle, Re 73
Merritt v Merritt 76
Nash v Inman 77
Nordenfelt v Maxim Nordenfelt Guns & Ammunition Co. 80
Parkinson v College of Ambulance Ltd and Harrison 83
Pearce v Brooks 84
Pharmaceutical Society of Great Britain v Boots Cash Chemists (Southern) Ltd 86
Phillips v Brooks 87

Pinnel's Case	89
Planché v Colburn	90
Raffles v Wichelhaus	91
Ramsgate Victoria Hotel Co. v Montefiore	92
Roberts v Gray	109
Simpkins v Pays	113
Stilk v Myrick	114
Taylor v Caldwell	117
Thomas v Thomas	118
Victoria Laundry (Windsor) Ltd v Newman Industries Ltd	119
Warner Bros Pictures v Nelson	121
Welch v Cheesman	122

LAW OF TORT

Baker v Hopkins Ltd	19
Beard v London General Omnibus Co.	21
Bernstein, Baron, of Leigh v Skyviews & General Ltd	23
Bliss v Hall	25
Bolton v Stone	26
Bourhill v Young	27
Byrne v Deane	28
Campbell v Paddington Borough Council	29
Cassidy v Daily Mirror Newspaper Ltd	31
Christie v Davey	34
Cope v Sharpe	38
Cutler v United Dairies Ltd	41
Donoghue (or M'Alister) v Stevenson	48
Hall v Brooklands Auto-Racing Club	55
Kelsen v Imperial Tobacco Co. Ltd	65
King v Phillips	66
Lampleigh v Braithwait	68
Limpus v London General Omnibus Co.	72
McLoughlin v O'Brian	74
Mahon v Osborne	75
National Coal Board v Evans & Co. and another	78
Nichols v Marsland	79
O'Connor v Swan & Edgar and Carmichael	81
Paris v Stepney Borough Council	82
Phipps v Rochester Corporation	88
Robinson v Kilvert	110
Sayers v Harlow Urban District Council	111
Storey v Ashton	115

Wagon Mound, The; Overseas Tankship (UK) Ltd v Morts Dock & Engineering Co. 120

CRIMINAL LAW

Director of Public Prosecutions v Newbury and Jones 46
R v Allen 93
R v Bowsher 94
R v Byrne 95
R v Church 96
R v Collins 98
R v Deller 99
R v Dudley and Stephens 100
R v Halliday 101
R v Lloyd, Bhuee and Ali 102
R v Miller 103
R v Morris 104
R v Nedrick 105
R v Quick 106
R v Tolson 107
Sweet v Parsley 116

LAW OF SUCCESSION

Jones, Re 63
K (Deceased), Re 64

FAMILY LAW

Hyde v Hyde 61

EMPLOYMENT LAW

Pepper v Webb 85

ALLCARD v SKINNER

Notes

(1887) 36 Ch D 145

THE FACTS The plaintiff entered a protestant Order known as 'The Sisters of the Poor'. Her vow of poverty required her to surrender her worldly possessions — some £7,000 — to the Order. Six years after leaving she sued for the return of the £1,671 which had not been spent by the Order, claiming that it had been obtained as a result of undue influence of the Lady Superior (the defendant).

THE DECISION The plaintiff had no opportunity of seeking external advice and so should have been able to recover the remaining money on the basis of undue influence, but her claim failed due to her six-year delay in bringing the action.

COMMENTARY Undue influence is a subtle form of pressure exerted by one party to the contract on the other such that the judgment of the party influenced is not freely exercised and their consent not freely given. It arises when the relationship of the parties to an agreement is not based on equality.

Where undue influence exists the contract is voidable at the option of the party influenced.

In the following relationships of trust there is a presumption of undue influence. This means that to escape liability the defendant must rebut the presumption, i.e., satisfy the court that undue influence was not, in fact, used. These relationships are:

(a) religious advisor and advisee (as above);
(b) doctor and patient;
(c) solicitor and client;
(d) teacher and pupil;
(e) parent and child;
(f) guardian and ward;
(g) trustee and beneficiary.

Notes: (i) The relationship of husband and wife is not included. (ii) It is an equitable principle, i.e., a concept that originated in that branch of law developed in the former Court of Chancery and known as 'Equity'. Since 'delay defeats equity' (known as the doctrine of laches) the court — as in this case — may refuse to grant relief.

Notes

APPLESON v LITTLEWOOD LTD

[1939] 1 All ER 464

THE FACTS The plaintiff sent in what he claimed was a winning football pools coupon entitling him to a prize of £4,335.

The defendant refused to pay, relying on a condition on the coupon which stated that: 'it shall not be attended by or give rise to any legal relationship, rights, duties, consequences . . .'.

THE DECISION The plaintiff's claim failed. The condition indicated that the defendants had no intention to create legal relations.

COMMENTARY There is a presumption that agreements of a domestic or social nature are not intended to be legally binding, whilst those of a business or commercial nature are intended to be legally binding.

These are not rules, merely presumptions, and presumptions can be rebutted, as in this case.

The arrangement between the parties appeared to be commercial in nature but the condition on the coupon operated to rebut the normal presumption and the transaction was not binding in law.

BAKER v HOPKINS LTD

Notes

[1959] 3 All ER 225

THE FACTS Hopkins Ltd were employed to clean out a well. It was decided to use a petrol-engined pump in the well and the two employees of Hopkins Ltd were instructed not to go down the well until all the engine fumes had cleared. However, both employees ignored this instruction, went down the well without waiting for the fumes to clear and were overcome by the fumes. Dr Baker was called to the well and he realised that if the lives of the two men were to be saved he could not wait for the arrival of the fire brigade, who had also been called. So Dr Baker had himself lowered on a rope down the well, only to find that the two men were already dead. The rope got caught and Dr Baker could not be raised out of the well in time to prevent him being overcome by the fumes as well.

Mrs Baker claimed in negligence for the loss of her husband, and Hopkins Ltd put up the defence of *volenti non fit injuria*, that is, that Dr Baker had consented to the risk of the harm that caused his death.

THE DECISION At first instance and on appeal it was held that, as Dr Baker was acting in the role of a rescuer, the maxim *volenti non fit injuria* was not applicable. Thus Mrs Baker's claim succeeded.

COMMENTARY This case illustrates that a rescuer is treated as a special case in English law, which has followed the law of the United States in this respect. Consequently, a rescuer cannot be regarded as having voluntarily accepted a risk of harm unless it would be wholly unreasonable to do so. Clearly any doctor in Dr Baker's position would have known that only very prompt action could prevent death from carbon monoxide poisoning.

BALFOUR v BALFOUR

[1919] 2 KB 571

THE FACTS The defendant, a Civil Servant on leave in England, was due to return with his wife, the plaintiff, to Sri Lanka (Ceylon) when she became ill.

Mrs Balfour had to remain in England and her husband promised her a household allowance of £30 per month.

Later, the couple separated and Mrs Balfour sued for the allowance.

THE DECISION The agreement was in the nature of a domestic agreement. It relied on bonds of trust and affection but was not binding in law. The plaintiff was not legally entitled to the £30 per month.

COMMENTARY For an agreement to be a contract the parties must have entered into it with 'the intention to create legal relations'. If this intention is absent, then the agreement is not legally binding, i.e., there is no contract.

This case illustrates the attitude the law takes towards agreements of a social or domestic nature; there is a presumption that such agreements are not intended to be legally binding. However, there are instances where the presumption does not apply; that is to say, there are cases where agreements which appear to be of a domestic character are legally binding. In such cases the presumption is said to be 'rebutted' (see, for example, *Simpkins* v *Pays*, p. 113).

BEARD v LONDON GENERAL OMNIBUS CO.

[1900] 2 QB 530

Notes

THE FACTS The driver of a bus left it at the terminus and the bus conductor then drove it in order to turn the bus around. During the turning process the bus struck and injured Beard, who claimed compensation from the London General Omnibus Co. as the employer of the bus conductor who was driving the vehicle at the time of the accident.

THE DECISION It was held by the Court of Appeal that the employer, London General Omnibus Co., was not liable to Beard for the actions of the bus conductor because their employee was not acting in the course of his employment as a bus conductor at the time of the accident.

COMMENTARY The vicarious liability of an employer for the wrongs done by his employees has always been limited to liability for wrongs done during the course of the employment (see *Storey* v *Ashton*, p. 115).

This case illustrates that the courts may take a rather narrow view of the meaning of the expression 'during the course of the employment'. It may be wondered why Beard should not just have claimed against the bus conductor rather than the employer, but generally the employer is in a much better position to pay any compensation that may be awarded. Now that third party insurance is required for all vehicle drivers, the injured party would proceed against the insurers as well.

Notes

BELL v LEVER BROS

[1932] AC 161

THE FACTS Bell was employed by Lever Bros as managing director of one of their subsidiary companies. The subsidiary company was subsequently involved in a merger and under a redundancy agreement Lever Bros contracted to pay Bell £30,000 as compensation. Later they discovered that Bell had engaged in secret trading, an activity for which he could have been dismissed without compensation. Lever Bros sought to recover the £30,000 on the ground that the redundancy agreement was void due to mistake.

THE DECISION Lever Bros were unsuccessful, because they had got what they had bargained for, i.e., the termination of Bell's contract of employment.

The fact that they could have released Bell from his contract on much cheaper terms indicated a mistake as to quality and such a mistake does not render the contract void.

COMMENTARY The general rule is *caveat emptor* (let the buyer beware). This means, for instance, that if a buyer of a painting misjudges the value of the work and pays too much, that is his fault. He made a mistake as to quality and this does not invalidate the contract.

Lever Bros paid more than was necessary to obtain a redundancy agreement releasing Bell from his contract of employment. They made a mistake as to quality, for they could have dismissed him summarily without any 'golden handshake'. The result is the same — the redundancy agreement is not invalidated and Bell can keep the money.

Note: the court decided there was no fraud involved in the redundancy agreement.

BARON BERNSTEIN OF LEIGH v SKYVIEWS & GENERAL LTD

Notes

[1977] 2 All ER 902

THE FACTS Without seeking permission, an aircraft belonging to Skyviews & General Ltd flew over Lord Bernstein's estate and took photographs of the house and grounds.

These photographs were subsequently offered for sale to Lord Bernstein, who sued in trespass on the basis that as owner of the land he was also the owner of the airspace above that land.

THE DECISION It was held that there was no trespass at common law as a landowner's rights to the airspace above his property did not extend to an unlimited height. The court declined to lay down a height to which ownership of the airspace extends, saying that it was limited to the height necessary for the ordinary use and enjoyment of the land and buildings. In the airspace above that height the landowner had no greater rights than anyone else.

It was also held that even if there was a common-law trespass, the provisions of the Civil Aviation Act 1949 prevented any action being taken in respect of that trespass. Section 40 of the 1949 Act provides:

> No action shall lie in respect of trespass or in respect of nuisance, by reason only of the flight of an aircraft over any property at a height above the ground, which having regard to the wind and weather, and all the circumstances of the case is reasonable . . .

COMMENTARY The limited ownership of the airspace above land in no way prevents landowners taking an action in trespass against signs, cranes and trees, etc., that invade their airspace. However, the landowner cannot take a trespass action against, say, a satellite that passes over his garden.

This case is a good example of common sense applied to the law. As the judge remarked, there being no law against the taking of photographs, Skyviews & General Ltd could take all the photographs they wished from outside the boundaries of Lord Bernstein's estate.

Notes

BISSET v WILKINSON

[1927] AC 177

THE FACTS The owner of farmland in New Zealand told a prospective purchaser of the farm that, in his opinion, it would 'carry 2,000 sheep'. The land had not previously been used as a sheep farm.

After buying the farm the purchaser discovered that it would only support a fraction of that number, so he sued for misrepresentation.

THE DECISION This was an honest statement of opinion which did not amount to a misrepresentation. The purchaser's claim failed.

COMMENTARY Misrepresentation is an untrue statement of fact which induces the contract, i.e., persuades the other party to enter the contract.

This case illustrates that a statement of belief or opinion cannot generally be a misrepresentation (assuming no fraud is involved). If the vendor in this case had said, 'It is a well-known fact that the land will support 2,000 sheep', he would have been liable in misrepresentation.

Note: silence cannot generally amount to misrepresentation. Suppose, for instance, that the vendor knew that the land was not suitable for sheep farming but did not say anything — there would be no misrepresentation. This reflects the general maxim *caveat emptor* (let the buyer beware). The effect is that a purchaser must make enquiries designed to elicit the information he needs to know. He should 'force' the vendor to make positive statements, e.g., 'The land will support 2,000 sheep.'

BLISS v HALL

(1838) 4 Bing NC 183

Notes

THE FACTS The plaintiff took up residence next to a tallow factory which for three years had manufactured candles.

The plaintiff sued in nuisance, complaining of the 'divers noisome, noxious and offensive vapours, fumes, smells and stenches' emitted by the factory.

THE DECISION There was an actionable nuisance. The plaintiff had a right to 'wholesome air' and it was no defence that the plaintiff came to the nuisance.

COMMENTARY Private nuisance is an unlawful interference with another's use or enjoyment of land, or some right over, or in connection with, it. Typical examples include noise, smoke, heat, smell, vibration, etc. It generally involves an element of repetition, e.g., one smoky bonfire does not entitle a neighbour to sue.

Lord Wright commented: 'A balance has to be maintained between the right of the occupier to do what he likes with his own, and the right of a neighbour not to be interfered with.'

Note: what is a nuisance in one area may not be a nuisance in another, e.g., a fish and chip shop may be a nuisance in a residential area but not in a commercial district. This is summed up in the dictum from the case *Sturges* v *Bridgman*, 'What may be a nuisance in Belgrave Square would not necessarily be so in Bermondsey.'

Nuisance is a wrong to occupation; it follows that a tenant can sue and be sued.

Notes

BOLTON v STONE

[1951] 1 All ER 1078

THE FACTS While standing in a public road adjacent to a cricket ground, Miss Stone was struck and injured by a cricket ball that had been hit out of the ground during a match. The cricket ground was enclosed by a fence which was effectively 17 feet high where it separated the ground from the public road.

It was established that a ball had only been hit out of the ground into the public road on six occasions in the previous 30 years and that these incidents had not caused any injury or damage.

Miss Stone claimed in negligence against the cricket club and at first instance the claim was dismissed. On appeal the Court of Appeal upheld the claim, so the cricket club appealed to the House of Lords.

THE DECISION In the judgment of the House of Lords, the standard of care in the law of negligence is the standard of the ordinarily careful man. The 'ordinarily careful man' does not take precautions against every foreseeable risk, only against risks which are reasonably likely to happen. Therefore the claim in negligence was dismissed.

COMMENTARY This case highlights the difficult point that mere foreseeability of harm does not always give rise to a duty of care in the law of negligence. To the test of 'is it foreseeable?' has to be added a further test, 'what is the risk of the event happening?' One of the Law Lords, Lord Reid, considered that a cricket ball escape on average once every five years was on the 'border line' of acceptable risk.

BOURHILL v YOUNG

Notes

[1943] AC 92

THE FACTS The plaintiff was eight months pregnant. She was alighting from a tram when she heard a collision in which a motorcyclist was killed. She did not see the accident but heard the collision and saw some blood on the road. She suffered nervous shock and gave birth to a stillborn child. Mrs Bourhill sued the personal representatives of the motorcyclist for his negligence.

THE DECISION The action failed as the injury to the plaintiff was not a reasonably foreseeable consequence of the motorcyclist's negligent driving.

COMMENTARY To be successful in an action in negligence the plaintiff must prove that the defendant:

(a) owed him a duty of care;
(b) was in breach of that duty;
(c) caused the injury to the plaintiff as a result.

A duty of care is owed to one's neighbour. In the tort of negligence a neighbour is anyone whom it may reasonably be anticipated will be affected by the act complained of.

The act complained of in this case was the motorcyclist's negligent driving which resulted in the fatal crash. He did not owe the plaintiff a duty of care since what happened could not have been anticipated, i.e., that a lady who did not see the accident would suffer nervous shock and give birth to a stillborn child.

Note: it is possible to recover damages for nervous shock in negligence. The case of *McLoughlin* v *O'Brian* (p. 74) illustrates that the courts are now prepared to make awards of damages for nervous shock to people who were not even at the scene of the accident.

Notes

BYRNE v DEANE

[1937] 2 All ER 204

THE FACTS A golf club provided illegal gaming machines for the use of the members. Someone informed the police of that fact and the gaming machines had to be removed. The following notice was put up in the place where the gaming machines had stood:

> For many years upon this spot
> You heard the sound of a merry bell
> Those who were rash and those who were not
> Lost and made a spot of cash
> But he who gave the game away
> May he byrnne in hell and rue the day

Byrne, a member of the club, claimed in defamation (libel), saying the words implied that he had informed the police, that he was disloyal, devoid of sporting spirit and not fit to be a member of the club; all of which damaged his reputation with other people.

At first instance Byrne was awarded nominal damages and costs, so the golf club appealed.

THE DECISION The Court of Appeal held that allegations of reporting unlawful actions to the police, whether true or false, cannot damage the reputation of a person in the opinion of 'right-thinking members of society'. Consequently Byrne had no claim in defamation.

COMMENTARY This case illustrates the basic defamation test, namely: does the allegation damage the reputation of the victim in the opinion of 'right-thinking members of society' and no one else.

CAMPBELL v PADDINGTON BOROUGH COUNCIL

[1911] 1 KB 869

Notes

THE FACTS The plaintiff let rooms overlooking the route for the funeral procession of King Edward VII. The defendants erected a stand which obstructed the highway and the view from the plaintiff's window. The plaintiff sued in the tort of public nuisance.

THE DECISION The plaintiff was entitled to damages for the profits which, but for the defentants' act, she would probably have made by letting rooms.

COMMENTARY Public nuisance is a crime. It becomes a tort as well where one person is affected more than the public in general.

The defendants in this case had obstructed the highway, which constitutes the crime of public nuisance. The plaintiff had been particularly affected and so could sue for the tort of public nuisance.

The classic type of public nuisance is interference with the public right of way along the highway, for example, by obstructing it or by making the way unsafe by erecting dangerous structures on or near the highway.

A plaintiff wishing to sue for the tort of public nuisance always has to show that he has suffered some special damage over and above that which is suffered by the public as a result of the nuisance, e.g., personal injury (a protruding lamp overhanging the highway fell and injured a passer-by), damage to property (maintenance to highway undermining foundations), loss of business profits (queues to theatre blocking entrance to shop), or inconvenience (loss of sleep due to traffic noise).

Notes

CARLILL v THE CARBOLIC SMOKE BALL CO.

[1893] 1 QB 256

THE FACTS Mrs Carlill read an advertisement for a patent medicine known as a carbolic smoke ball. The advertisement made claims that the product would cure a number of ailments, including influenza. A reward of £100 was offered to anyone who caught influenza after using the smoke ball as directed. A sum of £1,000 was said to have been deposited in a bank to show the makers' 'sincerity in the matter'.

Mrs Carlill bought the smoke ball, using it for eight weeks as directed, but she still caught influenza and so claimed the £100 reward. The makers refused to pay the reward to Mrs Carlill, who then sued on the promise of the reward. The makers raised several defences to the claim by Mrs Carlill, including:

(a) The reward offer was an attempt to contract with the entire world, which was not possible in English Law.

(b) The reward offer was a mere 'puff', there being no intention to enter into a binding legal obligation (no intention to create legal relations).

(c) Mrs Carlill had not communicated her acceptance of the reward offer.

THE DECISION Mrs Carlill was entitled to the £100 reward because:

(a) It was possible to make offers to the entire world where there was a promise by one party for an act by the other party (a unilateral contract).

(b) The deposit of the £1,000 showed an intention to pay claims.

(c) In unilateral contracts communication of acceptance was not necessary.

COMMENTARY This leading case establishes that in certain situations an offer, as well as an 'invitation to treat', can be made to the entire world. Thus 'price promise' offers, where a retailer offers a partial refund if his goods can be bought cheaper anywhere else within a certain time, can be enforced at law. This is the modern application of the *Carlill* case.

CASSIDY v DAILY MIRROR NEWSPAPERS LTD

Notes

[1929] 2 KB 331

THE FACTS The plaintiff was the wife of a man who was pictured with another woman in the defendants' newspaper under the heading 'Today's Gossip'. Beneath the picture was a statement that their engagement had recently been announced.

The plaintiff brought an action for defamation, claiming that there was an innuendo that she had been living 'in sin' with the man in the photograph, i.e., readers of the newspaper who knew her would conclude that if he had just become engaged to the woman in the photograph, he could not be married to her.

THE DECISION The photograph and statement were held to be defamatory of the plaintiff, since they contained the innuendo that she was not married to her husband. The plaintiff was awarded damages.

COMMENTARY An innuendo is a statement that is innocent on the face of it but which has a hidden defamatory meaning, e.g., 'Dr Brown drinks' might simply mean that the doctor likes mineral water but many people would draw the conclusion that the doctor drinks too much alcohol.

In cases where innuendo is claimed, it is up to the plaintiff to establish the hidden defamatory meaning.

Sometimes unintentional defamation occurs. This happens where a newspaper publishes an article that is true of one person but is taken to refer to another and is defamatory of him.

In general, a plaintiff wishing to be successful in an action for defamation must prove:

(a) that the statement was defamatory, i.e., that it lowered him in the estimation of other reasonably minded people;

(b) that the statement referred to him (or was taken by inference to refer to him, as in the above case);

(c) that the statement was published, i.e., communicated to a third person;

(d) that damage was suffered (in most cases).

Notes

CENTRAL LONDON PROPERTY TRUST LTD v HIGH TREES HOUSE LTD

[1947] KB 130

THE FACTS In 1937 the plaintiffs let to the defendants a block of flats at an annual rent of £2,500. The defendants in turn let each individual flat.

Following the outbreak of war the defendants found that they could not let all the flats and so the plaintiffs agreed in writing to a reduction in the annual rent of £1,250. No express time limit was set for the operation of this reduction. From 1940 to 1945 the defendants paid the reduced rent.

In 1945 the flats were full again and the plaintiffs brought an action claiming they were entitled to the original rent from 1945 onwards *and* submitting that they were entitled to the arrears of rent for the years 1940-1945. The basis of the claim was that there was no consideration for the agreement to reduce the rent, i.e., that it was a 'gratuitous waiver', which was not binding.

THE DECISION The plaintiffs were entitled to revert to the original rent from 1945 since the abnormal wartime conditions no longer applied.

However, Denning J was of the opinion that any submission that they were entitled to the arrears would be defeated by the doctrine of *equitable estoppel*.

COMMENTARY The case demonstrates how the doctrine of equitable estoppel may be applied to prevent someone going back on a 'waiver' (a promise to accept less than was originally owed). There are three conditions to be met before the doctrine will apply:

(a) The promisor must waive his legal rights (i.e., give up some legal entitlement).

(b) The waiver must be gratuitous (i.e., made for nothing).

(c) The other party must alter his position in reliance on the waiver.

If all three conditions are fulfilled the plaintiff is 'estopped', or prevented, from going back on his word even though it was a promise made for nothing.

Note: The doctrine of estoppel is equitable and is based on fairness, so it cannot be used by a defendant to escape liability where he virtually holds the plaintiff to ransom, e.g., 'take £X or you'll get nothing'.

CHAPLIN v LESLIE FREWIN (PUBLISHERS) LTD

Notes

[1966] Ch 71

THE FACTS The plaintiff, the estranged son of Charlie Chaplin, signed a contract with the defendants for the publication of his autobiography while he was still a minor. Later he tried to avoid the contract, claiming it was not binding on him.

THE DECISION The contract was valid and binding. It was a beneficial contract of service which would enable him to earn his living and support his family.

COMMENTARY There are two classes of contract which bind a minor:

(a) Necessaries (see *Nash* v *Inman*, p. 77).

(b) Beneficial contracts of service: these are contracts which, taken as a whole, benefit the minor. The fact that the contract contains a harsh term will not necessarily mean it is void; if the remaining terms are in the minor's best interest, e.g., by enhancing his future prospects, the contract is valid. Hence beneficial contracts of service often involve the minor in education, training, apprenticeship, etc. (see *Roberts* v *Gray* p. 109).

Note: the plaintiff in the above case was 19 when he made the contract. He was a minor because the age of majority was at that time 21. It was not until 1969 when the Famiy Law Reform Act was passed that the age of majority was reduced to 18. Prior to that piece of legislation anyone under the age of 21 was referred to, for contractual purposes, as an infant!

Notes

CHRISTIE v DAVEY

[1893] 1 Ch 316

THE FACTS The parties lived in adjoining semi-detached houses. The defendant, exasperated by the music lessons and musical parties given by the plaintiff, retaliated by knocking on the wall, banging metal trays, whistling and shrieking!

The plaintiff sued in the tort of nuisance.

THE DECISION The defendant had acted maliciously and was liable. The plaintiff was granted an injunction.

COMMENTARY This case illustrates that motive may be relevant in nuisance. The courts, in judging what constitutes a nuisance, take into consideration the purpose of the defendant's activity. Acts which might otherwise be justified, may be regarded as unreasonable and a nuisance if done out of an improper motive such as malice or spite.

North J, in the above case, observed, 'if what has taken place had occurred between two sets of persons both perfectly innocent, I should have taken an entirely different view of the case'.

Consequently the mental state of the defendant may make his conduct nuisance, although had that mental state been different, nuisance would not have been committed. For example, a defendant who encouraged his son to discharge guns on his land with the intention that the noise would interfere with the breeding of the plaintiff's silver foxes was held liable in nuisance.

Note: the law recognises that a certain amount of discomfort is inevitable in life owing to the activities of one's neighbours but also expects that neighbours will lessen this discomfort as much as they are able, i.e., there must be a certain amount of 'give and take'.

CHRISTIE v DAVEY

'retaliated by knocking on the wall, banging metal trays . . .'

Notes

COLLINS v GODEFROY

(1831) 1 B & Ad 950

THE FACTS The plaintiff had received a subpoena requiring him to attend court as a witness for the defendant. The defendant promised to pay him six guineas. The defendant subsequently refused to pay and the plaintiff sued.

THE DECISION The plaintiff was unsuccessful. In attending court, he was only doing what he was already legally obliged by the subpoena to do. Consequently he was not providing any consideration in exchange for the defendant's promise to pay — so the agreement was not binding.

COMMENTARY Consideration is a necessary element in the formation of a valid simple contract. The classic definition of consideration was expressed in the case of *Currie* v *Misa* as 'some right, interest, profit or benefit accruing to one party, or some forbearance, detriment, loss or responsibility given, suffered or undertaken by the other'. In other words, it is the exchange value in the contract — both parties must 'give up' or sacrifice something in exchange for what they receive.

It follows that a promise to perform an existing duty is not consideration since nothing has been 'sacrificed'. Collins had not sacrificed anything as he had to attend court — regardless of the six guineas. If he had not received the subpoena then his time and trouble in attending court would have been his consideration.

Vague promises, e.g., 'to do the right thing', do not constitute consideration, likewise agreements made 'in consideration of natural love and affection'.

CONDOR v THE BARRON KNIGHTS LTD

Notes

[1966] 1 WLR 87

THE FACTS The plaintiff was a drummer in the Barron Knights band. He had a five-year contract which required him to play on seven nights a week when the band had engagements. He fell ill and was advised by his doctor that he was only fit to play on four nights a week. Consequently the band terminated his contract of employment.

THE DECISION The contract was frustrated (brought to an end/discharged). In the business sense it was impossible for the plaintiff to continue his contract so it was properly terminated.

COMMENTARY A contract is frustrated when the contract has become impossible to perform. When this happens the party who has been prejudiced is released from his legal obligation to fulfil the contract.

This case illustrates that one of the events that may frustrate a contract is personal injury in a contract for personal services.

Contracts discharged on this ground have included: an agreement to perform at a concert; an agreement to serve an apprenticeship of a fixed duration.

Note: (i) Frustration of contract may be referred to as supervening or subsequent impossibility. (ii) A contract is not frustrated merely because it has become more difficult to fulfil the contract (see *Davis Construction Ltd* v *Fareham Urban District Council*, p. 42).

COPE v SHARPE
[1912] 1 KB 496

THE FACTS A fire broke out on the plaintiff's land. The defendant, a gamekeeper, entered his land and lit some heather to create a 'fire break' to protect nesting pheasants belonging to his employer. The plaintiff sued in trespass.

THE DECISION The defence of necessity applied and the gamekeeper was not liable. There was a real and imminent danger to the game and what he did was reasonably necessary.

COMMENTARY Necessity is one of the general defences to an action in tort. It applies where the defendant reasonably responds to a danger by taking action intended to prevent a greater peril, e.g., destroying a building damaged by fire to prevent its collapse on to the highway.

The necessity must be judged at the time of the defendant's action. In the above case the gamekeeper's action was justified by the circumstances at the time even though the fire actually died out before reaching his employer's land.

Necessity may, in certain circumstances, be a justification for inflicting harm on a person. In *Leigh* v *Gladstone* it was decided that prison warders who forcibly fed the plaintiff, a suffragette on hunger strike in prison, were not liable for the tort of battery.

Similarly, a surgeon who performs a life-saving operation without obtaining consent may claim this defence.

COUTURIER v HASTIE

Notes

(1853) 156 ER 43

THE FACTS Hastie, merchants in Smyrna, sent a cargo of corn by sea from Salonica to England. Couturier, in London, was employed as an agent to resell the corn on the basis that he would make good any loss due to default in the resale contract (a *del credere* agent).

Couturier sold on the corn, while it was in transit, to Callender. It was then discovered that the corn had been sold en route by the captain of the ship when the corn became overheated. Callender then repudiated the contract of sale on the basis that at the time of sale to him the corn no longer existed. Thus Couturier could become liable to Hastie for the purchse price promised by Callender.

THE DECISION At first instance it was held that the contract of resale for the corn was valid. On appeal to the Court of Appeal (subsequently affirmed by the House of Lords) it was held that there was no valid contract of resale, as at the time of contracting, unknown to the parties, the corn had ceased to exist as such.

COMMENTARY Note that this case had its title reversed in the course of progress through the courts, starting as *Hastie* v *Couturier*.

In this rather confusing case it should be borne in mind that Couturier, as the reselling agent, could be liable for the default of the purchaser if the contract he arranged with the purchaser, Callender, was held valid. This old case is often cited as authority for the proposition that a mistake about the existence of the subject-matter of a contract results in there being no contract, as the parties are not in true agreement.

CUNDY v LINDSAY

(1878) 3 App Cas 459

THE FACTS A rogue named Blenkarn ordered goods by post from the defendants, signing the order 'Blenkiron & Co.', a genuine company known to the defendants.

Blenkarn received the goods and sold them to Cundy.

Lindsay & Co. successfully sued Cundy for the return of the goods. Cundy appealed.

THE DECISION There had been an operative mistake as to the identity of the other party (Blenkarn). Such a mistake renders the contract void. Since the contract between Blenkarn and Lindsay & Co. was void, Cundy could not obtain legal title, i.e., ownership of the goods, for title cannot pass under a void contract.

COMMENTARY Mistakes take many forms.

Certain mistakes render the contract void. These are known as 'operative' mistakes. A mistake that does not affect the validity of a contract is known as an 'inoperative' mistake.

A mistake as to the identity of the other party to a contract may be operative or inoperative.

The general rule is that where the parties are dealing on a 'face to face' basis, the contract will not be void for mistake, merely voidable for misrepresentation.

This case demonstrates that where the parties are not dealing on a face to face basis, e.g., through the post, the original contract (Blenkarn/Lindsay & Co.) *is* void for mistake, so any subsequent contract (Blenkarn/Cundy) cannot pass title to the goods, i.e., ownership remains with the party who was the victim of mistaken identity (Lindsay & Co.).

CUTLER v UNITED DAIRIES LTD

Notes

[1933] 2 KB 297

THE FACTS The plaintiff was injured whilst trying to pacify a milkman's horse which had bolted into a field. He sued for negligence.

The defendants sought to rely on the defence *volenti non fit injuria* ('no injury can be done to a willing person' or 'he who consents cannot complain').

THE DECISION The defence was successful.

The plaintiff's action failed, as he had voluntarily undertaken the risk and the hazards that went with it.

COMMENTARY The defence in the law of tort known as *volenti* can be used against a volunteer or rescuer who is injured whilst attempting a rescue.

The defence will not be successful where the rescuer was acting under a moral or legal duty to preserve life, e.g., a doctor (see *Baker* v *Hopkins Ltd*, p. 19) or a policeman (*Haynes* v *Harwood*).

In the *Cutler* case, the plaintiff was merely a bystander alerted by the milkman's cries for help in a situation which presented no danger to others. In the *Haynes* case, the plaintiff was a policeman who was attempting to stop a runaway horse in a crowded street.

Notes

DAVIS CONTRACTORS LTD v FAREHAM URBAN DISTRICT COUNCIL

[1956] 2 All ER 145

THE FACTS In 1946 Davis offered to build 78 houses for Fareham Council in eight months for £92,425 subject to adequate labour and material supplies being available. The subsequent formal contract between the parties contained no mention of the offer term regarding the availability of labour and material. Due to labour and material shortages the houses took 22 months to complete and the cost increased by £17,651.

Davis claimed that their offer term about availability of labour and material was incorporated in the formal contract although not expressly stated in writing; also that the contract was frustrated by the delay, consequently they could recover the additional cost (£17,651) as an extra to the contract price (£92,425) which was no longer binding on them.

THE DECISION At first instance it was held that the offer term was a term of the formal contract and that Davis could recover the additional cost. On appeal to the Court of Appeal (subsequently affirmed by the House of Lords) it was held that the offer term was not incorporated in the formal contract, that the extra cost could not be recovered and that the contract was not frustrated by the delay.

COMMENTARY The House of Lords when considering what events frustrate a contract made it clear that difficulties resulting from the delayed performance of a contract do not frustrate the contract if those difficulties could have been readily anticipated and provided for, as in this case.

DE FRANCESCO v BARNUM

(1890) 45 Ch D 430

Notes

THE FACTS The defendant, a 14-year-old girl, entered into a contract with the plaintiff to be taught stage dancing. The contract stipulated that she would not marry during the contract and that she would not accept professional engagements without the plaintiff's permission.

THE DECISION The contract was void.

It was not a beneficial contract of service. Whilst it was in the nature of an apprenticeship, the terms were so harsh (onerous) that 'the child was at the absolute disposal of the plaintiff'. It could not therefore be regarded as beneficial.

COMMENTARY Where a minor enters into a 'beneficial contract of service' it is binding on him, i.e., it is a valid contract which can be enforced by him and against him. Contracts for education, training or apprenticeship generally fall within this category.

This case demonstrates, however, that such contracts must be looked at as a whole. If the contract is predominantly in the minor's best interest then, despite an isolated onerous term, it is binding on him. If, on the other hand, it is predominantly harsh then, despite a beneficial aspect (such as being taught stage dancing), it is not binding.

Notes

DERRY v PEEK

[1886-90] All ER Rep 1

THE FACTS The Plymouth, Devonport & District Tramway Co. operated horse-drawn trams under a private Act of Parliament. The Act provided that, subject to the approval of the Board of Trade, steam or mechanical trams could be used.

The directors of the Tramway Company offered shares for sale, their prospectus stating: 'One great feature of this undertaking, to which considerable importance should be attached, is that, by special Act of Parliament obtained, the company has the right to use steam or mechanical motive power, instead of horses, and it is fully expected that by this means a considerable saving will result . . .'. Sir Henry Peek, acting in reliance on this statement, bought shares in the Tramway Company.

Later the Board of Trade refused consent to the use of steam or mechanical power, the Company was wound up and the shareholders lost money. Sir Henry sued the directors for fraudulent misrepresentation, claiming that the statement in their prospectus had induced him to buy shares in the Company. At first instance the claim was rejected but on appeal the Court of Appeal upheld the claim, so the directors further appealed to the House of Lords.

THE DECISION It was held that a misrepresentation was only fraudulent if:

(a) it was made knowing that it was untrue; *or*
(b) it was made without belief in its truth; *or*
(c) it was made recklessly, that is, not caring if it was true or false.

Whilst the prospectus was inaccurate, the directors honestly thought that the Board of Trade consent was a formality, so their misrepresentation was not fraudulent. The House of Lords reversed the decision of the Court of Appeal — the directors were not liable to Sir Henry Peek.

COMMENTARY This is one of the leading cases on fraudulent misrepresentation but the circumstances are not likely to recur, since directors who issue a prospectus now have a statutory duty for its accuracy under the Companies Acts.

DICKINSON v DODDS

(1876) 2 Ch D 463

Notes

THE FACTS On 10 June 1874 Dodds delivered by hand to Dickinson a written offer to sell certain properties. The offer stated: 'This offer to be left over until Friday, 9 o'clock a.m. June 12 1874.' During the afternoon of 11 June Dickinson was informed by an estate agent that Dodds was in negotiations with another person for the sale of the properties.

At 7.00 p.m. on 11 June Dickinson delivered to the residence of Dodds, by hand, a letter of acceptance for the properties, which it seems was never seen by Dodds. At 7.00 a.m. on 12 June the estate agent, acting for Dickinson, delivered to Dodds personally a duplicate written acceptance by Dickinson for the properties. It then transpired that Dodds had contracted with the other person for the sale of the properties on the afternoon of 11 June.

At first instance Dickinson was awarded a decree of specific performance against Dodds (an order to Dodds to sell the properties to Dickinson). Dodds appealed.

THE DECISION The Court of Appeal held that the order of specific performance should be set aside, as it must have been perfectly obvious to Dickinson before he accepted the offer from Dodds that Dodds had changed his mind and might be contemplating offering his properties to another. Thus Dickinson had notice, through a third party (the estate agent) that the offer by Dodds was revoked. The fact that Dickinson did not receive notice of revocation directly from Dodds was not material.

COMMENTARY This case answers a question about which there is often misunderstanding, namely that in the law of contract a promise which is made gratis (i.e., for nothing) cannot be enforced unless made under seal.

Dickinson did not buy the promise by Dodds to keep the offer open until a certain time; it would have been very different if Dickinson had paid Dodds for his promise, for then Dickinson would have had a binding option to purchase the properties.

It is unwise to rely on any promise given gratis, especially one involving the sale of property.

Notes

DIRECTOR OF PUBLIC PROSECUTIONS v NEWBURY AND JONES

[1976] 2 All ER 365

THE FACTS The guard of a local train from Pontypridd to Cardiff was sitting next to the driver. As the train approached a bridge over the line Newbury and Jones (both aged about 15) pushed a large piece of concrete off the parapet of the bridge. The piece of concrete hit the front of the driver's compartment of the train, killing the guard.

Newbury and Jones were convicted of manslaughter and the conviction was upheld on appeal by the Court of Appeal. Newbury and Jones further appealed to the House of Lords on the grounds that a person could not be convicted of manslaughter if he did not foresee the harm his action might cause; that is, he did not foresee that the action was dangerous.

THE DECISION The House of Lords held that persons who carry out unlawful and dangerous acts which harm others are liable for manslaughter if their action results in death.

Foresight of the risk of harm to others is not material. How dangerous the action in question may be is to be decided by the objective test — would the 'man in the street' have recognised the action as dangerous — not did the wrongdoer recognise that action as dangerous. The conviction was upheld.

COMMENTARY This case illustrates the 'unlawful and dangerous act' type of manslaughter.

Note that there are two elements in such cases, namely: an unlawful act which is also a dangerous act *in the view of the man in the street* and not in the view of the wrongdoer. The unlawful act in this case was, of course, attempting to obstruct the rail track contrary to British Rail by-laws.

DONOGHUE v STEVENSON

'a glass of ginger beer'

Notes

DONOGHUE (OR M'ALISTER) v STEVENSON

[1932] AC 562

THE FACTS A lady was given a glass of ginger beer to drink, which had been poured out of an opaque glass type of bottle, thus preventing the contents from being seen. Later, when the rest of the ginger beer was poured from the bottle, the contents were seen to be contaminated with the decomposing remains of a dead snail.

The realisation by the lady that she had consumed contaminated ginger beer caused her nervous shock and subsequent gastric illness. A claim for compensation for the negligence of the manufacturer of the ginger beer was rejected at first instance and on appeal, so there was a further appeal to the House of Lords.

THE DECISION By a majority the House of Lords held that:

> Every person has a legal duty of care to avoid acts or omissions which can reasonably be foreseen as likely to injure a 'neighbour'.

It was also held that, in law, a 'neighbour' is any person who could be so affected by the act (or omission) that they ought reasonably to be in the mind of the doer of that act (or omission) when it is thought about. The claim for compensation was upheld.

COMMENTARY This is the leading case on negligence and has already become one of the most important judicial decisions of the century. From this very ordinary situation the principle was established that all persons may owe a legal duty of care not to do anything that can be foreseen as likely to harm others.

It is essential to note that the extent of the duty of care is limited by the test of *foreseeability of harm*; where the harm could not have been foreseen it is said to be 'too remote'.

In this case also note that the injured party was *given* the ginger beer, so there was no contractual relationship with either the seller or the manufacturer of the contaminated ginger beer, consequently no claim in contract was possible.

Many providers of services now attempt to limit liability for their negligence, sometimes by international agreement, as in the case of the airlines. Such limitations are subject to statutory controls.

ESSO PETROLEUM v HARPER'S GARAGES LTD

Notes

[1967] 1 All ER 699

THE FACTS Harper's owned two garages, each of which sold petrol and oils, etc. In 1962 and 1963 Harper's entered into agreements with Esso that only Esso petrol and oils would be purchased for sale at both garages ('solus' agreements). One agreement was to run for 4½ years and the other agreement was to run for 21 years. During 1964 Harper's began to sell other brands of petrol and oils at both garages, so Esso sought an injunction to prevent Harper's from breaking their 'solus' agreements.

Injunctions were granted at first instance but set aside on appeal by the Court of Appeal on the grounds that the 'solus' agreements were in restraint of trade and illegal. Esso further appealed to the House of Lords.

THE DECISION The House of Lords held that agreements that restrain trade are only enforceable if the restraint could be justified.

The purpose of the 'solus' agreements so far as Esso was concerned was to ensure a stable system of distribution for their products, and this was a legitimate interest that Esso were entitled to protect for a reasonable length of time.

In the opinion of all of the members of the House of Lords 4½ years was a reasonable length of time for a 'solus' agreement to operate but 21 years was an unreasonable length of time for such an agreement to run. The injunction was restored in respect of the 4½ year agreement, and the setting aside of the injunction was confirmed in respect of the 21 year agreement.

COMMENTARY This leading case indicates that some restraint of trade provisions in agreements are lawful and do not render such agreements void. In the case of garages it should be borne in mind that petrol suppliers often provide financial assistance to the garage owner in return for a 'solus' agreement covering the supply of petrol and oils, etc.

Notes

FELTHOUSE v BINDLEY

(1862) 142 ER 1037

THE FACTS The plaintiff wrote offering to buy his nephew's horse for £30 and added: 'If I hear no more about him, I consider the horse mine at that price.' The nephew did not reply but did instruct the defendant, an auctioneer, to withdraw the horse from a forthcoming sale of his stock. The defendant did not do so and the horse was sold at auction to a third party.

The plaintiff sued the auctioneer in the tort of conversion.

THE DECISION The plaintiff had not contracted to buy the horse, as 'silence cannot amount to acceptance'. It followed that the horse did not belong to the plaintiff, so he could not sue the auctioneer for conversion.

COMMENTARY This is an instance where a principle in the law of contract determined the outcome of a case in another branch of law, namely the tort of conversion. Conversion is an unjustifiable interference with another's ownership of goods.

The plaintiff would only succeed if he demonstrated that his ownership had been interfered with. He failed as he did not have ownership. This was established by the application of the contractual principle that 'silence cannot amount to acceptance', i.e., he could not claim that his offer of £30 for the horse had been accepted, for his nephew's silence could not, in law, be regarded as acceptance.

This case may be distinguished from *Carlill* v *The Carbolic Smoke Ball Co. Ltd* (p. 30). In the *Carlill* case the *defendants* dispensed with the need to communicate acceptance, i.e., an offeror may dispense with the need to communicate acceptance but he may not — as in *Felthouse* v *Bindley* — arbitrarily impose contractual liability upon an offeree merely by proclaiming that silence shall be deemed consent.

FISHER v BELL

Notes

[1961] 1 QB 394

THE FACTS The defendant displayed a flick-knife with a price tag attached in his shop window. It was a criminal offence to 'offer for sale' certain offensive weapons, including flick-knives.

The defendant was prosecuted.

THE DECISION The defendant was acquitted. He had not 'offered for sale' the flick-knife, as its display was merely an invitation to treat. An invitation to treat is not an offer, simply an invitation to the other party to make an offer.

COMMENTARY This is an instance where a principle in the law of contract determined the outcome of a case in another branch of law, namely criminal law.

The court could not convict the defendant, as he did not come within the wording of the offence, i.e., he had not *offered* for sale the flick-knife since its display was, in law, an invitation to treat.

Other examples of an invitation to treat include:

— goods on 'self-service' shelves;
— newspaper advertisements;
— TV advertisements;
— an auctioneer asking for bids;
— transport timetables;
— wine lists.

Notes

FITCH v DEWES

[1921] 2 AC 158

THE FACTS A solicitor's managing clerk took employment with a Tamworth firm of solicitors for three years; the contract of employment contained the following term: 'The managing clerk shall not be engaged or manage or be concerned in the office, profession, or business of a solciitor within a radius of 7 miles of the Town Hall of Tamworth.'

On leaving this employment the managing clerk sought to challenge the validity of the term as being in restraint of trade, since being without any time limit it amounted to a life-long prohibition on him working in Tamworth.

THE DECISION Although unlimited in time, the restriction would be enforced, as it did not exceed what was reasonably required to protect the 'trade secrets' (identity, etc., of clients) of the employing solicitors and the restriction was not contrary to the public interest.

COMMENTARY This decision is still relied upon; many firms of solicitors employ their staff on condition that they do not work for any other firm of soliitors within the seven-mile radius.

It is unusual for terms in restraint of trade to be unlimited in time but perhaps the legal profession is a special case, as so many clients of established firms of solicitors have placed their legal work with the same firm for very many years.

FOSTER v MACKINNON

(1869) LR 4 CP 704

Notes

THE FACTS The plaintiff was the holder of a bill of exchange for £3,000 which had been endorsed by the defendant.

The defendant had been induced to sign the bill by a third party named Callow, who told him that it was a guarantee.

The bill was later negotiated to the plaintiff who took it in ignorance of the fraud. He sued the defendant as endorser of the bill.

THE DECISION The plaintiff was unsuccessful. The defendant was not liable on the bill.

An old man of feeble sight, he had not been negligent in signing the bill. The document he signed was fundamentally different from the document he thought he was signing, so the defence of *non est factum* applied.

COMMENTARY *Non est factum* means 'it is not my act/deed'. This defence is based on the principle that a contract is not binding where the essential ingredient of consent is lacking.

The plea of *non est factum* is only available within narrow limits. The defendant must establish that:

(a) The document which he signed was fundamentally different as regards character or effect from the document he thought he was signing (a bill of exchange is different in character from a guarantee).

(b) He was not careless (Mackinnon, being senile and poor-sighted, was held not to have been negligent).

Notes

HADLEY v BAXENDALE

(1854) 9 Ex 341

THE FACTS The crankshaft of the plaintiff's mill broke. He employed the defendant, a carrier, to take it to a manufacturer to copy it and make a new one. The defendant took longer than necessary to return the new crankshaft, during which time the mill was idle.

The plaintiff sued for loss of profits.

THE DECISION The loss was 'too remote', i.e., the defendant was not liable for he could not reasonably have foreseen the loss, as it was usual for a mill owner to have a spare crankshaft. The plaintiff had not informed the defendant that there was any urgency.

COMMENTARY A plaintiff cannot recover *all* losses arising from a breach of contract. Only those losses which are attributable to the breach are recoverable. Any other loss is said to be 'too remote'.

This case established the principles which are applied to determine whether or not a loss is recoverable. A plaintiff can recover damages for a loss that either:

(a) arises naturally from the breach (it did not in the *Hadley* case, for a mill owner would usually have a spare crankshaft); *or*

(b) ought reasonably to have been in the contemplation of both parties as the likely result of the breach (it was not in the *Hadley* case, as the mill owner did not explain the urgency of the situation).

Losses which fall into neither category are 'too remote' and damages cannot be recovered.

A good illustration of the application of this rule is shown in the case *Victoria Laundry (Windsor) Ltd* v *Newman Industries Ltd* (see p. 119).

HALL v BROOKLANDS AUTO-RACING CLUB

Notes

[1933] 1 KB 205

THE FACTS The plaintiff, a spectator, was injured after two cars collided on the race track, causing one of them to crash through the railings. Two other spectators were killed. It was the first accident of its kind for 23 years.

The plaintiff sued in the tort of negligence.

THE DECISION The defence of *volenti non fit injuria* applied.

The plaintiff was not entitled to damages because this kind of danger to spectators was inherent in the sport and he was taken to have assented to the risk of such an accident.

COMMENTARY *Volenti non fit injuria* is one of the general defences available in an action in tort.

This Latin expression translates as 'no injury can be done to a willing person' or 'he who consents cannot complain'. It means that if a person voluntarily undertakes a task which involves risk, he is generally given to have accepted that risk and so cannot afterwards complain if he is injured — providing the precautions taken by a defendant were adequate in the circumstances. In this particular case the protective iron railings were 4.5 ft from the track and accidents of this type were a rare event.

Note: a spectator does not consent to negligence on the part of participants in a game or sport but 'provided the competition or sport is being performed within the rules and the requirement of the sport and by a person of adequate skill and competence, the spectator does not expect his safety to be regarded by the participant'.

Notes

HARRIS v NICKERSON

(1873) 21 WR 635

THE FACTS Nickerson, an auctioneer, advertised in the London newspapers that an auction sale of brewing equipment and office furniture, etc., would be held in Bury St Edmunds on a certain day. Nickerson also issued catalogues listing the various items to be offered for sale. Harris attended the auction sale, intending to bid for items of office furniture, but these lots were withdrawn from the sale.

Harris sued Nickerson for compensation for his loss of time and at first instance was awarded £2 12s 6d (£2.62½ pence). Nickerson appealed.

THE DECISION The Queen's Bench Court held that the advertisements of the auction and the catalogues of the lots did not amount to an offer to sell from which a binding contract with all the persons attending the auction sale could be inferred.

Harris was not entitled to any compensation.

COMMENTARY This case demonstrates the distinction in the law of contract between an offer and a declaration of intention. Whilst an offer is capable of giving rise to a contract upon a valid acceptance, a declaration of intent cannot do so.

It would be impractical for auctioneers to ensure that every person who read their advertisements, etc., received prior notice of the withdrawal of any advertised lot. The conditions of sale used by most auctioneers usually provide that any item advertised for sale can be withdrawn without notice.

HARVEY v FACEY

Notes

[1893] AC 552

THE FACTS The following telegrams were exchanged between the prospective purchaser (the plaintiff) and the owner (the defendant) of a piece of land known as 'Bumper Hall Pen':

'Will you sell us Bumper Hall Pen? Telegraph lowest cash price.'

'Lowest price for Bumper Hall Pen, £900.'

'We agree to buy Bumper Hall Pen for £900 asked by you.'

The owner refused to sell. The prospective purchaser sued, claiming that there was a contract between himself and the owner.

THE DECISION The second telegram was not an offer but only an indication of what the defendant would accept if he resolved to sell. As it was not an offer, the third telegram could not be an acceptance, i.e., there was no contract between the parties.

COMMENTARY This case illustrates that an offer must be firm. The courts are reluctant to treat a statement as an offer capable of acceptance unless the statement appears definite.

The second telegram could more accurately be described as a statement of price rather than a definite offer to sell.

Note: Special rules apply to the sale of land.

An agreement to sell land must be in writing or 'evidenced in writing'.

Normally a formal contract is drawn up and exchanged. Sometimes, however, a 'note or memorandum' of the agreement is sufficient to create legal relations, provided that it contains all the material terms of the contract.

Notes

HEDLEY BYRNE & CO. LTD v HELLER & PARTNERS LTD

[1964] AC 465

THE FACTS The plaintiffs made enquiries concerning the creditworthiness of a company called Easipower, in response to which the defendants (Easipower's bankers) gave favourable references. In reliance on this, the plaintiffs incurred expenditure on Easipower's behalf and, when Easipower went into liquidation, they suffered substantial loss (£17,000).

They sued the defendants in the tort of negligence.

THE DECISION The court of first instance and the Court of Appeal found for the defendants, i.e., decided that they were not liable.

The House of Lords decided that the reference was negligent and wrong and the defendants would have been liable in negligence had the reference not been given 'without responsibility on our part', i.e., the disclaimer protected the defendants so they were not liable.

COMMENTARY This case established that a person could in principle be liable for negligent words (called negligent misstatement) as well as negligent acts. In the event the defendants escaped liability because of a disclaimer of responsibility.

Liability for negligent misstatement arises where:

(a) the person making the statement has a special knowledge or skill (e.g. a banker);

(b) he knew the other party relied on these qualities (e.g., an investor);

(c) the other party suffers a loss as a result of such reliance (e.g., loss of investment).

HENTHORN v FRASER

[1892] 2 Ch 27

Notes

THE FACTS The secretary of a Liverpool land society handed to Henthorn a written offer to sell, for £750, some houses belonging to the society. At about noon the following day the secretary of the society posted to Henthorn a notice withdrawing the offer to sell the houses. This notice was delivered to Henthorn's home in Birkenhead shortly after 5.00 p.m. the same day. Meanwhile Henthorn had posted an acceptance of the offer at 3.50 p.m. some 1 hour 10 minutes before receipt of the notice of revocation of the offer. Henthorn's acceptance was delivered to the offices of the society after they had closed, so it was not read until the next day.

Henthorn sought an order of specific performance to compel the society to complete the sale of the houses to him (the remedy normally given for the breach of a contract for the sale of land — see *Hyde* v *Wrench*, p. 62). At first instance the order for specific performance was refused. Henthorn appealed.

THE DECISION The Court of Appeal held that where the circumstances are such that it must have been within the contemplation of the parties that, according to the ordinary usages of mankind, the post might be used as a means of communicating the acceptance of an offer, the acceptance is complete as soon as it is posted.

Thus the contract for the sale of the houses was complete on the posting of the acceptance by Henthorn about 1 hour 10 minutes before he received notice of the revocation of the offer (which must be communicated to be effective).

Henthorn was entitled to an order for specific performance.

COMMENTARY This decision follows an earlier one by the House of Lords that where the parties chose the post to communicate offer and acceptance, any acceptance is binding on posting ('the postal rule'). This rule is one of convenience, and if the offeror does not wish to be bound without immediate notice he can specify in his offer that he will require actual notice of acceptance if postal communication is used. Alternatively the offeror can specify some instant form of communication. Thus the offeror can avoid the problems of the postal rule if he wishes.

Notes

HOUSEHOLD FIRE INSURANCE CO. v GRANT

(1879) 27 WR 858

THE FACTS Grant made an application to purchase 100 shares at £1 each in the Household Fire Insurance Co. and paid a deposit of 1 shilling per share to the company's bankers. Grant also agreed to pay the balance of the cost of the shares (19 shillings per share) within 12 months of the date of the allotment of shares to him.

The secretary of the Household Fire Insurance Co. made out a letter of allotment and posted it to Grant. Grant never received the letter of allotment. Later Grant was asked to pay the balance of the cost of his shares but he refused to do so.

THE DECISION Both at first instance and on appeal to the Court of Appeal it was held that Grant was a shareholder and liable to pay for the balance of the cost of his shares. The contract between Grant and the Household Fire Insurance Co., for the purchase of the shares became binding the moment the acceptance of Grant's offer was posted by the secretary to the company.

COMMENTARY This case illustrates the 'postal rule' in the law of contract — a posted acceptance binds on posting even if never received. As was pointed out in the Court of Appeal, if a person making an offer requires *actual* communication of any acceptance of his offer, he is entitled to make this a condition of his offer or alternatively to specify in his offer a means of communication for any acceptance that is more certain than the ordinary post, for example recorded delivery, telex, etc.

HYDE v HYDE

(1861-73) All ER Rep 175

Notes

THE FACTS As the name suggests, this was a case in family law involving a husband and wife.

THE DECISION This case is not remarkable for the decision but for a description given by Lord Penzance which is generally accepted as the definition of marriage, namely:

> The voluntary union for life of one man and one woman to the exclusion of all others.

COMMENTARY It follows from the definition that:

(a) Forcible marriage and marriage by deceit or mistake are void, i.e., are of no legal effect.

(b) Marriages celebrated under English law are monogamous — 'one man and one woman'. Polygamous marriages, e.g., where a man marries more than one woman, may be recognised under English law but only if they fulfilled the laws of the country in which the marriage was celebrated.

(c) English law does not recognise marriage between persons of the same sex.

(d) The parties commence the marriage with the intention that it should be 'for life'. A divorce does, however, terminate the marriage and the parties are then free to remarry. A judicial separation does not terminate the marriage but terminates the duty to cohabit as man and wife.

(e) Adultery violates the definition — 'to the exclusion of all others'. It is therefore one of the five facts that will support a petition for divorce.

HYDE v WRENCH

(1840) 49 ER 132

THE FACTS Wrench wrote to Hyde offering to sell his farm to Hyde for £1,000. Agents acting on behalf of Hyde called on Wrench and said that Hyde would be willing to purchase the farm for £950. Wrench said that he wished to consider the matter for a few days. Subsequently Wrench wrote to Hyde saying that he was not prepared to sell the farm for £950. Two days later Hyde wrote saying he 'accepted' the offer by Wrench to sell the farm for £1,000 but Wrench had not renewed his offer. Hyde then brought an action for an order of specific performance (an order to carry out a contract); Wrench contested the action.

THE DECISION No contract existed between the parties for the sale of the farm.

The offer by Hyde of £950 amounted, in law, to a rejection of the offer by Wrench to sell the farm for £1,000 and it was not open to Hyde to accept the original offer by Wrench after rejection.

There being no contract between the parties for the sale of the farm, no order of specific performance could be made.

COMMENTARY This old case remains the authority for the proposition that a counter-offer terminates an original offer and if the original offeror does not wish to renew the offer he need not do so; also that to be effective the acceptance of an offer must be unconditional.

The concept that a contract is a bargain is reflected in this decision. The risk of 'haggling' over the contract price or other terms of the contract is clear; if the 'haggle' does not come off the 'haggler' risks losing the deal, as the original offeror need not renew his offer if he does not want to do so.

RE JONES

[1981] Fam 7

Notes

THE FACTS Jones was a soldier serving in Northern Ireland. He had made a formal will leaving his property to his mother. In 1978 he was shot and on the way to hospital, and in the presence of two officers, said, 'If I do not make it, make sure Anne gets all my stuff.' Anne was his fiancée. Jones died the following day.

The court had to decide whether the statement constituted a valid informal will, replacing the earlier will in favour of his mother.

THE DECISION The statement was accepted as his last will.

COMMENTARY Under normal conditions, a will must be in writing, signed by the testator (the person making the will) and witnessed by at least two persons. In certain emergencies or in wartime, however, it is not always possible to comply with the strict rules for making a will, e.g., witnesses may not be available.

The law therefore grants special privileges to soldiers, sailors and airmen on active military service and to sailors at sea. An informal or 'nuncupative' will may be made by such persons, provided they have reached the age of 14. If the will is in writing, no witnesses are needed. If made orally there must be someone present who can later testify as to the deceased's wishes. This is what happened in the above case.

Note: an informal will remains valid even after the hostilities or emergency has ended and after the testator has left the armed forces or ceased to be a sailor.

Notes

RE K (DECEASED)

[1985] 1 All ER 403

THE FACTS Mr and Mrs K were married in 1974 and Mrs K had been subjected to considerable matrimonial violence but continued to live with her husband. In September 1982 Mr K was killed by the discharge of a shotgun held by his wife, who was convicted of manslaughter and placed on probation.

In his will Mr K had left the residue of his estate worth about £400,000 to Mrs K for her life and then to four other persons (residuary legatees, i.e., persons entitled to share the remainder of an estate after all the bequests have been satisfied). The residuary legatees objected to Mrs K taking her life interest on the grounds that she should not benefit from her criminal act. Mrs K contended that the Forfeiture Act 1982, which became law two weeks after she killed her husband, had retrospective effect, so that a court now had a discretion whether or not to allow her to benefit by her late husband's will.

The executor of K's will applied to the Chancery Division of the High Court for a determination.

THE DECISION It was held that Mrs K had been a loyal wife who had suffered grave violence and it would be unjust to prevent her taking the benefits her late husband had conferred upon her. Accordingly, Mrs K would be allowed to take her life interest.

COMMENTARY This was the first case involving the provisions of the 1982 Forfeiture Act. Before 1982 the forfeiture rule was based on public policy (the interests of the community). The rule was that a person who had unlawfully killed should not benefit from the act. As in many matrimonial disputes, the violence in *Re K* was not entirely one-sided and the effect of the 1982 Act is to require the court to form a view of the moral culpability of the parties before the exercise of the statutory discretion to set aside the rule.

KELSEN v IMPERIAL TOBACCO CO. LTD

Notes

[1957] 2 All ER 343

THE FACTS Mr Kelsen rented a tobacconist's shop and Imperial Tobacco Co. had an advertising sign attached to the wall of the adjoining property so that the sign projected about 8 inches into the airspace above Mr Kelsen's shop. The only access to the sign was from Mr Kelsen's premises and he had allowed employees of Imperial Tobacco Co. entry from time to time for cleaning and repair of the sign.

After a business dispute between the parties Mr Kelsen gave Imperial Tobacco Co. notice to remove the sign in so far as it invaded his airspace, subsequently taking an action in trespass for an injunction to require the removal of the sign from his airspace.

THE DECISION The court had first to decide if the lease of the shop to Mr Kelsen included the airspace above. The judge found 'nothing in the lease which displaces the prima facie conclusion which one would otherwise reach that the airspace above the demised premises is a part of the premises conveyed'. (Demised means leased.)

Consequently, in law, Mr Kelsen as the 'tenant' of the airspace above the shop had the right to exclude others and an injunction would be granted to require the portion of the sign projecting into Mr Kelsen's airspace to be removed within 28 days.

COMMENTARY Whilst the motive for the action may be open to some doubt, the decision provides authority for treating an invasion of the airspace immediately above a property as though it were an invasion of the property itself, notwithstanding that there is no damage to the interests of the occupier of the property.

This sort of minor invasion of an airspace can happen when a roof gutter overhangs a boundary, but it may be wise to suffer the trespass rather than the rain-water.

For trespass to airspace refer also to *Baron Bernstein of Leigh* v *Skyviews & General Ltd* (p. 23).

KING v PHILLIPS
[1953] 1 All ER 617

THE FACTS Mrs King was looking out of an upstairs window towards the street when she heard a scream and saw Phillips' taxicab reversing over her child's tricycle but the child could not be seen. As Mrs King was running into the street she met her child, who was unharmed. Mrs King claimed compensation for the nervous shock she had suffered due to the negligence of the taxicab driver, Mr Phillips.

At first instance Mrs King lost her claim for compensation. She appealed.

THE DECISION The Court of Appeal held that in the law of negligence the extent of the duty of care not to cause harm was limited by the test of the foreseeability of the harm and that this included harm caused by nervous shock.

No reasonable driver, even if driving in a manner that caused damage to property, would have anticipated the harm suffered by Mrs King.

Refusal of claim for compensation was upheld.

COMMENTARY The decision in this case followed the decision in *Bourhill* v *Young* (p. 27).

It should be noted that what Mr Phillips could have foreseen is not the test, which is an objective one, namely, what could any reasonabe driver in those circumsances have foreseen.

One problem with claims for nervous shock is that the claimant may be some distance away from the occurrence. For example, if a person on a ladder picking apples from his tree is startled by, say, the sound of a collision between two cars and suffers a nervous shock causing him to drop the apples, ought this to be a sufficient basis to found a claim against the negligent driver of one of the crashed cars?

KRELL v HENRY
[1903] 2 KB 740

Notes

THE FACTS In June 1902 Henry saw an advertisement that a flat (56A Pall Mall), with windows overlooking the route of the forthcoming coronation procession of King Edward VII on 26 and 27 June, was to let for those two days. Henry agreed, in writing, to pay £75 rent for the use of the flat on those two days and paid a deposit of £25 in advance, the balance of the rent being due for payment on 24 June.

On 24 June the coronation of the King was cancelled due to his illness. Henry refused to pay the balance of the agreed rent for the flat, so Krell sued for this sum. At first instance the claim by Krell failed. He appealed.

THE DECISION The Court of Appeal held that the purpose of the agreement for the use of the flat, namely the viewing of the coronation procession on 26 and 27 June, failed without either party being at fault. Although this purpose was not mentioned in the agreement between the parties, it must have been in their contemplation at the time of contracting.

Henry was not liable for the balance of the agreed rent. (Henry did not pursue a claim for the return of his £25 deposit.)

COMMENTARY This case, one of the 'coronation cases', raises the question, 'What did Henry buy — rooms with a view of a coronation procession, or merely rooms with a view?' Had the possibility of cancellation of the coronation been fully considered before the parties contracted, might not Krell have said, 'The hirer must take the risk, I cannot guarantee that the coronation procession will take place or even pass my premises.' The Law Reform (Frustrated Contracts) Act 1943 now regulates situations such as occurred in this case.

Notes

LAMPLEIGH v BRAITHWAIT

(1615) Hob 105

THE FACTS The defendant was convicted of murder and requested the plaintiff to do all he could to get a pardon for him from the king. The plaintiff did so successfully, whereupon he was promised £100 by the reprieved man (the defendant). The money was never paid, so the plaintiff sued on the basis that the defendant was legally obliged to pay. The outcome depended on whether the service provided by the plaintiff amounted to valid consideration.

THE DECISION The plaintiff was entitled to the £100. He had provided consideration by 'journeying to and from London and Newmarket' at his own expense and this consideration was valid as the services were performed in response to the defendant's request.

COMMENTARY The general rule is that consideration must not be 'past' — 'past consideration is no consideration'. This means that an act performed in the past is not consideration for a promise made in the present, e.g., suppose A repairs B's car as a favour after which B promises A £20 for his trouble. If the money is not paid, A cannot obtain it as what he did (repair B's car) was past at the time B promised to pay and past consideration is no consideration. It can be represented as follows:

A repairs B's car . . . . after which . . . . B promises A £20 (past consideration)

Lampleigh v *Braithwait* is an exception to the general rule that past consideration is no consideration. The distinguishing feature is that the defendant *requested* the service. The court considered that the request implied that the service would ultimately be paid for — the previous request and the subsequent promise to pay for it were treated as part of the same transaction. It can be represented as follows:

1. Request to obtain pardon
2. Lampleigh obtains pardon
3. Braithwait promises £100

The promise to pay 'attaches' to the request, therefore the obtaining of the pardon is not 'past'.

LEAF v INTERNATIONAL GALLERIES

Notes

[1950] 2 KB 86

THE FACTS In 1944 the plaintiff bought a picture from the defendants which they both honestly believed had been painted by the artist Constable. In 1949 the plaintiff discoverd that it was not a genuine Constable and he claimed rescission on the ground of innocent misrepresentation.

THE DECISION The plaintiff's action failed. There had been an innocent misrepresentation but the lapse of five years (1944-1949) was sufficient to bar the plaintiff's right of rescission — even though he had not previousy discovered the misrepresentation.

COMMENTARY A misrepresentation is a false statement of fact that induces a contract. An innocent misrepresentation occurs where the false statement has been made in the honest belief that the statement is true — as in this case.

The party misled can bring an action for rescission. This amounts to a request that the parties be restored to their original positions (i.e., pre-contractual).

However, it is a discretionary remedy and the court may refuse to grant it if there is a long time delay between the innocent misrepresentation and the application of rescission — as here. 'It behoves the purchaser either to verify or, as the case may be, to disprove the representation within a reasonable time, or else stand or fall by it.'

Note: The court considered the legal effect of the mistake that had occurred concerning the subject-matter of the contract (the painting), but decided that it amounted to a mistake 'as to quality' and this was insufficient to render the contract void.

LEAF v INTERNATIONAL GALLERIES

'it was not a genuine Constable'

LEWIS v AVERAY

[1971] 3 All ER 907

Notes

THE FACTS Lewis advertised his car for sale and a man who answered the advertisement agreed to buy the car for £450. The purchaser said he was Richard Green the actor and offered Lewis a cheque in payment for the car which was signed 'R. A. Green'. The purchaser wanted to take the car away at once and Lewis asked for some proof that the purchaser was R. A. Green, the actor. The purchaser produced a film studio pass in the name of 'Richard A. Green' which carried a photograph of the purchaser. Lewis, after inspecting this evidence of identity allowed the car to be taken away at once in exchange for the cheque.

The car was sold by 'Green' to Averay without delay for cash, and when Lewis found the cheque he had accepted in payment for his car was dishonoured he traced the car to Averay and claimed it back. The man representing himself as 'Richard Green' had vanished (with, of course, Averay's cash).

THE DECISION Where a transaction takes place between persons who are 'face to face' there is a presumption that the offer by one person (in this case Lewis) is made to the other person and not to any person that other person claims to be, unless it is clear from the negotiations leading up to the transaction that the transaction is only to be with the represented person and no one else. Thus Lewis offered to sell his car to an unknown person (a rogue) and not Richard Green. Consequently the rogue obtained a good title to the car until Lewis sought to avoid the transaction for non-payment, by which time the rogue had passed his title in this car to Averay.

The car was thus the legal property of Averay. The claim by Lewis failed.

COMMENTARY The presumption of dealing with the person actually present and not who that person claims to be can be rebutted if it is made very clear in the negotiations that the deal is with and only with the represented person. Merely checking a film studio pass is clearly not sufficient. Rogues come prepared with this type of identity 'evidence' to match the stolen cheque book they want to use. Perhaps it is safer never to sell to strangers for a cheque.

Notes

LIMPUS v LONDON GENERAL OMNIBUS CO.

(1862) 1 H & C 526

THE FACTS A bus driver obstructed the plaintiff's bus, causing a collision which damaged it. He had received specific printed instructions not to obstruct other buses. The plaintiffs sued the bus driver's employer, claiming they were vicariously liable for the damage.

THE DECISION The defendants were vicariously liable, for the driver was doing what he was employed to do and it made no difference that he was doing it in a way he was told not to.

COMMENTARY The term 'vicarious liability' is used to describe the situation where one person is liable for the wrongdoings of another. For an employer to be vicariously liable for the torts of his employee it must be shown that the employee was acting 'in the course of his employment'. An employee is within the course of his employment if he is doing what he was employed to do — even if he is doing it improperly or in a way which was forbidden.

The employer will not be liable if the employee is acting outside the course of his employment, e.g., if he is on 'a frolic of his own', such as taking a detour whilst on company business to visit a friend.

Note: In 1900 the defendants were involved in another case which can be contrasted with the above (see *Beard* v *London General Omnibus Co.*, p. 21).

Re McARDLE
[1951] 1 All ER 905

Notes

THE FACTS In his will McArdle directed that his wife, if she survived him, could live in his house for the remainder of her life (a tenant for life) but then the property was to be shared between his children. After McArdle died his widow lived in the house and spent £488 on alterations and improvements to the property.

When the work had been completed all the children who would eventually inherit the property signed a document which stated: 'In consideration of your carrying out certain alterations and improvements to the property, we hereby agree that the executors shall repay to you from the estate, when distributed, the sum of £488 in settlement of the amount spent on such improvements.'

Subsequently, the executors of McArdle's will refused to pay the £488.

THE DECISION The Court of Appeal held that the document signed by all the children was not a binding contract as Mrs McArdle had not given good consideration for the promise to repay the £488, since at the time of signing the document all the work of alteration and improvement to the house had been completed. Thus the consideration provided by Mrs McArdle for the repayment promise was past consideration.

COMMENTARY This case demonstrates the rule in the law of contract that 'past consideration is no consideration'.

In general, the other party's promise cannot be bought by a promise to do something that has already been done *unless the act has been requested* (see *Lampleigh* v *Braithwait*, p. 68). The McArdle children never asked their mother to spend money on alterations and improvements to what would become their house; Mrs McArdle acted on her own initiative.

Notes

McLOUGHLIN v O'BRIAN

[1983] 1 AC 410

THE FACTS Mr McLoughlin and his three children aged 2, 7 and 17 were injured in a road accident caused by the negligence of O'Brian, and they were taken to hospital. A motorist who had seen the accident went to the family home about two miles away and told Mrs McLoughlin what had happened, afterwards taking her to the hospital. On arrival at the hospital Mrs McLoughlin was told that her daughter, aged two, had died of her injuries and she saw her injured husband and other children before they had received any treatment for their injuries. As a result Mrs McLoughlin suffered severe and persisting nervous shock and claimed compensation from the negligent driver.

At first instance the claim was rejected on the grounds that Mrs McLoughlin's nervous shock was not reasonably foreseeable. On appeal (the Court of Appeal) the claim was also rejected on the grounds that a duty of care could only be imposed in relation to persons who were in close proximity to the negligent act, notwithstanding that the injury might be reasonably foreseeable.

Mrs McLoughlin further appealed to the House of Lords.

THE DECISION The test of liability for nervous shock was the reasonable foreseeability of the injury happening as a result of negligence. Accordingly Mrs McLoughlin was entitled to compensation; the fact that she was not at or near the scene of the road accident was not material.

COMMENTARY This decision by the House of Lords is of considerable significance and may indicate a change in judicial attitudes towards claims for nervous shock arising as a result of negligence.

The facts raise the question of possible liability by the hospital in allowing a close relative to see untreated, badly injured persons which it could be said is almost certain to cause nervous shock to that relative.

Note: The arbitrators for nervous shock claims by survivors of the *Herald of Free Enterprise* accident in 1987 have ruled that to qualify for compensation a nervous shock must give rise to a recognised psychiatric illness such as Post Traumatic Stress Disorder (PTSD) or 'pathological' grief.

MAHON v OSBORNE

[1939] 2 KB 14

Notes

THE FACTS A swab was found in the plaintiff's body during an operation. It had been left there by the defendant (a surgeon) following a previous operation.

THE DECISION The defendant was liable in the tort of negligence.

COMMENTARY This case is used to illustrate the application of the latin maxim *res ipsa loquitur* (the thing speaks for itself).

The maxim applies to situations where the inference of negligence is irresistable, i.e., the accident in question is one which would not ordinarily occur unless those in charge failed to exercise proper care, e.g., where two trains collide on the same railway line.

If the plaintiff successfuly raises the plea of *res ipsa loquitur*, the burden of proof switches to the defendant to prove he was not negligent. Lord Denning in another case illustrated it as follows:

> A plaintiff is entitled to say, 'I went into hospital to be cured of two stiff fingers, and my hand is useless. That should not have happened if due care had been used. Explain it, if you can.'

Unless the defendant can exonerate himself, the plaintiff is entitled to judgment. The defendant will be exonerated if he shows how the accident actually occurred and if this true explanation is consistent with due care on his part. Alternatively, he may prove that there was no lack of care on his part or on the part of anyone for whom he is responsible.

Notes

MERRITT v MERRITT

[1970] 2 All ER 760

THE FACTS Mr Merritt left the matrimonial home which he jointly owned with Mrs Merritt subject to a building society mortgage. Later, the parties had a meeting in Mr Merritt's car during which he agreed to pay Mrs Merritt £40 per month on condition that she paid the mortgage repayments out of this sum. Mrs Merritt refused to leave the car until the agreement was recorded in writing, so Mr Merritt wrote out the following statement and signed it: 'In consideration of the fact that you will pay all charges in connection with the house until such time as the mortgage repayment has been completed I will agree to transfer the property into your sole ownership.'

After Mrs Merritt had completed all the mortgage repayments Mr Merritt refused to transfer the house to his wife. Mrs Merritt sued on the agreement and the question for the court was whether or not the parties had made a domestic agreement, which would not be binding, or a contract, which could be enforced.

THE DECISION An agreement between a husband and wife is normally a domestic agreement and there is no intention to enter legal relations, i.e., no intention that any promise can be enforced.

Here the parties, although married, were not living in amity and might not rely upon 'honourable understandings', so it was to be assumed that they intended to create legal relations in their agreement; consequently the agreement between Mr and Mrs Merritt was a contract enforceable at law.

COMMENTARY This case vividly illustrates the danger of anyone, married or not, entering into agreements without advice from a solicitor, law centre or citizens advice bureau. If Mr Merritt had not bound himself, the division of the jointly owned property, if decided by a court, might have resulted in a different outcome.

The case can be used to show the essential difference between a domestic agreement and a contract.

NASH v INMAN

[1908] 2 KB 1

Notes

THE FACTS The defendant, a minor, ordered a quantity of clothing (including 11 fancy waistcoats) from the plaintiff, a tailor. When the clothes were delivered the defendant refused to pay the bill of nearly £123. The tailor sued for the money.

THE DECISION The tailor's action failed. The defendant's father (an architect) showed that his son had plenty of clothes suitable to his standard of living, i.e., the clothes supplied by the tailor were 'non-necessaries', therefore the minor was not obliged to pay.

COMMENTARY The common law provides that contracts made by minors for necessaries supplied, e.g., food, clothing, housing, transport, are enforceable. On the other hand, contracts with minors for 'non-necessaries' are not enforceable.

This case illustrates that even something as basic as clothing can be a non-necessary if the minor already had an adequate supply of the items concerned. Two questions must therefore be answered:

(a) Is the article concerned capable of being a necessary — 'articles of mere luxury are always excluded, though luxurious articles of utility are in some cases allowed'.

(b) Is the article concerned a necessary in the particular cirucmstances, e.g., if the defendant had been a poor student ordering a warm overcoat it would probably have been a necessary with the result that the student would have to pay!

Notes: (i) Where a minor fraudulently obtains goods (e.g., by lying about his age), he may be compelled to return them. (ii) Traders dealing with minors can protect themselves by insisting on a guarantor. The guarantor (usually a parent or guardian) undertakes that, if the minor fails to meet all or any of the payments, he will pay the trader. The Minors Contracts Act 1987 provides that such guarantees are binding even if made in connection with contracts that are unenforceable against the minor, e.g., where the contract is for a 'non-necessary'.

Notes

NATIONAL COAL BOARD v EVANS & CO. AND ANOTHER

[1951] 2 KB 861

THE FACTS Power to the plaintiffs' mine was cut off when an excavator operated on behalf of the defendants cut through an electric cable. The plaintiffs sued in trespass and negligence.

THE DECISION The defence of inevitable accident applied. The defendants were not liable as neither they nor the landowners knew of the existence of the cable and it was not marked on any available map.

COMMENTARY Inevitable accident is one of the general defences to an action in tort, i.e., a defence available to a defendant in every action where appropriate. If successful, it justifies or excuses the defendant's action and he is not liable.

Inevitable accident refers to the situation where something happens which could not have been avoided by taking ordinary precautions, i.e., the precautions a reasonable man could be expected to take. A reasonable man is not expected to guard against every eventuality—'People must guard against reasonable probabilities but they are not bound to guard against fantastic possibilities.'

Cases involving inevitable accident are rare. Generally the burden of proof is already on the plaintiff, e.g., in negligence the plaintiff must establish the defendant's lack of care. If he cannot do so, the defendant is not liable.

Thus in *Stanley* v *Powell*, another case used to illustrate inevitable accident, the defendant was not liable for injury to the plaintiff which occurred during a shoot when one of the defendant's shots glanced off the bough of a tree and struck the plaintiff. The court considered the defendant had not been negligent and that the injury was inflicted accidentally.

NICHOLS v MARSLAND

(1876) 2 Ex D 1

Notes

THE FACTS For many years Miss Marsland had had several artificial ornamental lakes on her estate, which had been formed by damming up a natural stream. Following an extraordinary rainfall said to be 'greater and more violent than any within living memory', the walls of the lakes collapsed under the weight of water and the rush of escaping water into the natural stream carried away four bridges over the stream that were the responsibility of Nichols.

Nichols claimed the cost of replacing the bridges from Miss Marsland, who contested liability.

THE DECISION Miss Marsland was held not to be liable for the loss of the four bridges, which was caused by an extraordinary act of nature that Miss Marsland could not have been expected to anticipate.

COMMENTARY This decision suggests that a person cannot be liable for situations arising from what are often called 'acts of God'. An 'act of God' may be regarded, in law, as a process of nature not due to the act of man. The accepted modern criterion for 'acts of God' is whether or not human foresight and prudence could reasonably recognise the possibility of the particular process or nature occurring.

The correctness of the decision in this case is therefore now open to doubt, for the criterion applied in the case was whether or not the event was reasonably to be anticipated.

Reasonable anticipation of an event is not at all the same thing as prudent foresight of the *possibility* of that event happening. In England it may not be reasonable to anticipate say, a hurricane, but nevertheless it cannot be said that there is no possibility of such an event.

Notes

NORDENFELT v MAXIM NORDENFELT GUNS & AMMUNITION CO.

[1894] AC 535

THE FACTS The plaintiff was an inventor and a manufacturer of guns and ammunition. He sold his business and entered into a contract with the defendants agreeing that for a period of 25 years he would not carry on a similar business anywhere in the world.

A dispute arose and the validity of the restraint was brought into question.

THE DECISION Although contracts in restraint of trade are prima facie (at first sight) void, this agreement was reasonable in the circumstances and binding between the parties.

COMMENTARY A contract in restraint of trade is one which restricts a person in the carrying on of his trade or business. Though prima facie void, the courts will enforce them if they are:

(a) reasonable between the parties;
(b) reasonable, having regard to the interests of the public.

In this case both conditions were satisfied:

(a) The plaintiff had been adequately compensated in return for giving up his manufacturing rights.
(b) The agreement increased exports.

Note: Contracts in restraint of trade fall into three categories:

1. Contracts between the buyer and seller of a business (as above).
2. Contracts between an employer and employee — restraining an employee from competing with his employer when he leaves (see *Fitch* v *Dewes*, p. 52).
3. Contracts between traders/distributors regulating conditions of trade, including so called 'solus trading agreements' whereby one party agrees to sell or distribute the goods of one manufacturer only (see *Esso Petroleum* v *Harper's Garages Ltd*, p. 49).

O'CONNOR v SWAN & EDGAR AND CARMICHAEL

Notes

[1963] 107 SJ 215

THE FACTS Mrs O'Connor was employed by Swan & Edgar, the former department store in London, as a sales assistant. Whilst at work in the store Mrs O'Connor was struck and injured by a section of ceiling that fell down.

Mrs O'Connor, being on the premises for a lawful purpose and thus in law a 'visitor', sued Swan & Edgar as occupiers under the provisions of the Occupiers' Liability Act 1957. The Act provides that occupiers shall have a 'common duty of care' to take such care as in all the circumstances of the case is reasonable to see the visitors will be reasonably safe in using the premises for the purposes for which they are invited.

Swan & Edgar together with the ceiling contractor, Carmichael, as co-defendant, sought to rely on the following provision of the 1957 Act:

> Where damage is caused to a visitor by a danger due to a faulty execution of any work of construction, maintenance or repair by an independent contractor employed by the occupier, the occupier is not to be treated without more as answerable for the danger if in all the circumstances he had acted reasonably in entrusting the work to an independent contractor and had taken such steps (if any) as he reasonably could in order to satisfy himself that the contractor was competent and that the work had been properly done.

THE DECISION It was held that Carmichael was liable as the occupier's independent competent contractor.

COMMENTARY It is essential to bear in mind that if an occupier is to avoid liability under the 1957 Act for the work of another, then it is up to the occupier to ensure as far as he can that his contractor is competent. Occupiers should have this in mind when having work done on their premises by relatives and friends, etc., which might subsequently injure a visitor.

Notes

PARIS v STEPNEY BOROUGH COUNCIL

[1951] 1 All ER 42

THE FACTS In 1942 Paris, who had lost the sight of one eye, took temporary employment with Stepney Council as a garage mechanic. In 1946 Paris was refused permanent and pensionable employment on account of his disability and in 1947 was given notice that his temporary employment was to be terminated. Two days before the notice expired Paris was working under a vehicle when a piece of metal injured his good eye, resulting in the loss of the sight in the good eye with the consequence that Paris became blind.

Paris claimed in negligence on the basis that his employer, Stepney Council, had failed in their duty of care for employee's safety in that the Council had not provided protective eye visors for use by employees and had not required employees to wear such visors.

THE DECISION At first instance Paris was awarded damages but on appeal the Court of Appeal set aside the award of damages, so Paris further appealed to the House of Lords.

By a 3/2 majority the House of Lords held that a careful employer must not merely take account of the degree of risk of injury to employees but must also have regard to the gravity of the consequences of such injury. The award of damages was restored, as the Council ought to have realised, at least from the time permanent employment was refused, that an eye injury to a one-eyed employee might have much more serious consequences than the same eye injury would have for a normally sighted employee.

COMMENTARY The rather unusual facts of this case provided the House of Lords with the opportunity to expand the duty of care in the law of negligence so that the level of the duty will vary with the circumstances.

PARKINSON v COLLEGE OF AMBULANCE LTD AND HARRISON

Notes

[1925] 2 KB 1

THE FACTS The secretary of the defendant charity fraudulently represented to the plaintiff that the charity was in a position to secure a knighthood for him — if he made an adequate donation. The plaintiff paid £3,000 to the charity but no knighthood was forthcoming, so he sued for the return of his money.

THE DECISION The plaintiff was unable to recover the money as the contract was illegal and void.

COMMENTARY Any contract that tends to promote corruption in public life is illegal and void. A void contract is no contract at all, i.e., it is not legally binding and the parties to it generally have no redress.

Persons in 'public life' in this context include civil servants, judges, army personnel, etc.

So if a civil servant obtained promotion by promising his superior a sum of money, the agreement between them would be illegal and void. Bribery and corruption are not a good basis for securing the interests of the nation; as one writer commented, 'all such contracts must have a material influence to diminish the respectablity, responsibility and purity of public officers and to introduce a system of official patronage, corruption and deceit wholly at war with the public interests'.

Note: Although the plaintiff had been deceived into believing that the charity was capable of securing a knighthood, the judge concluded that the plaintiff must have known that the whole arrangement was illegal.

Notes

PEARCE v BROOKS
(1866) 14 WR 614

THE FACTS Pearce was a coach-builder who supplied, on hire, to Brooks a brougham (a closed carriage). Brooks was a known prostitute. When Brooks failed to pay the hire charges for the brougham Pearce brought an action to recover the hire charges.

A jury was asked to decide whether Brooks used the brougham for the purposes of her trade as a prostitute and, if so, did Pearce know that this was the purpose for which the brougham was hired?

THE DECISION It was found that the brougham was used by Brooks as 'a part of her display to attract men' and that Pearce was fully aware of that fact. Consequently the contract of hire was void as being for an immoral purpose. Pearce was unable to recover the hire charges.

COMMENTARY This case supports the view that contracts for immoral purposes cannot exist as they are void.

Over the years there has been much speculation about what was displayed in the brougham to attract men.

PEPPER v WEBB

Notes

[1969] 1 WLR 514

THE FACTS Pepper was employed as head gardener by Major Webb. He worked satisfactorily for three months but then his attitude deteriorated. When asked about the arrangements for the greenhouse during the defendant's absence, Pepper replied, 'I couldn't care less about your bloody greenhouse or your sodding garden', and walked off.

He was dismissed summarily, i.e., on the spot, without being given any notice.

Pepper complained that the dismissal was unfair.

THE DECISION The dismissal was justified.

The plaintiff's conduct and his previous bad behaviour indicated an intention to repudiate the contract of employment.

COMMENTARY The Employment Protection (Consolidation) Act 1978, as amended by the Employment Act 1980, provides that an employee has the right not to be unfairly dismissed. Since the 1980 Act it is for an industrial tribunal to decide whether or not the employer acted reasonably.

Certain types of misconduct justify dismissal. They include insolence, persistent laziness, immorality, dishonesty and drunkenness. The misconduct will justify summary dismissal if it directly interferes with the business of the employer, or the employee's ability to perform his services.

One isolated incident of misconduct will not justify summary dismissal, e.g., in *Wilson* v *Racher* a gardener was dismissed for swearing at his employer on one occasion. This was considered to be an exceptional outburst from an otherwise competent and diligent employee who had been provoked by his employer. Therefore there were no grounds for dismissal.

Notes

PHARMACEUTICAL SOCIETY OF GREAT BRITAIN v BOOTS CASH CHEMISTS (SOUTHERN) LTD

[1953] 1 All ER 482

THE FACTS The defendants were prosecuted for infringing a provision of the Pharmacy and Poisons Act 1933 which made it unlawful to sell any listed poison 'unless the sale is effected under the supervision of a registered pharmacist'.

Their shop was selfservice and the customer had selected from the shelves a medicine covered by the Act and had taken it to the cash desk where a registered pharmacist was present.

THE DECISION The display of articles on the shelves was an invitation to treat. The customer made the offer when he presented the goods for payment and there was no 'sale' until his offer to buy was accepted at the cash desk. Since there was a registered pharmacist at the point of sale no offence had been committed.

COMMENTARY This is an instance where a principle in the law of contract determined the outcome of the case brought in another branch of law.

It illustrates the point that an invitation to treat is not an offer and cannot be accepted. It is an invitation to the other party to make an offer.

It involves the same principle as the later case, *Fisher* v *Bell* (p. 51) and, like that case, demonstrates the literal way in which the courts interpret the wording of an Act of Parliament.

PHILLIPS v BROOKS LTD

[1919] 2 KB 243

Notes

THE FACTS A man named North went into a jewellers' shop owned by Phillips and selected items of jewellery to a value of £3,000, making out a cheque in payment. When signing the cheque with a false name North said, 'You see who I am, I am Sir George Bullough', and gave an address in St James' Square. Phillips had heard of Sir George Bullough and on checking that the address given by North was the correct one for Sir George Bullough he offered to let North take the jewellery away with him, to which North replied that Phillips had better have the cheque cleared first but as it happened he would like to take a diamond ring away with him as it was for his wife's birthday the next day. Phillips then allowed North to have the ring, valued at £450.

When the cheque for £3,000 was dishonoured North was traced and convicted of obtaining the ring by false pretences but North had immediately pawned the ring for £350 with Brooks Ltd and disposed of the money.

Phillips claimed the return of the ring from Brooks Ltd.

THE DECISION Phillips, in fact, contracted to sell and deliver the ring to the person who came into his shop, who was not Sir George Bullough but a man in the name of North. Hence North obtained good title to the ring until such time as Phillips sought to avoid the contract of sale for non-payment. So North, having pawned the ring before non-payment was discovered by Phillips, could pass a good title to Brooks Ltd, who were entitled to retain the ring if the pledge was not redeemed.

COMMENTARY This case illustrates the presumption in the law of contract that in 'face to face' contracts there is an intention to contract with the person *actually present* and not who the person says he or she is.

The presumption can be set aside, but only if a party makes it absolutely clear that the identity of the other party is to be a condition of contracting.

Shopkeepers are not normally interested in the identity of their customers except as a possible indication of ability to pay. So the mistake by Phillips was about an attribute of his customer (the ability to pay).

Notes

PHIPPS v ROCHESTER CORPORATION

[1955] 1 QB 450

THE FACTS The plaintiff, a boy aged five, was out blackberrying with his sister, aged seven, and they walked across a building site being developed by the defendants. The defendants had dug a trench on the site 9 feet deep by 2½ feet wide. The earth had been heaped to a height of about 4 feet on one side. The plaintiff fell in and broke his leg.

THE DECISION The defendants were not liable because they could not anticipate that a child of this age would not be accompanied by a responsible person and so had not broken their duty of care.

COMMENTARY An occupier of land is under a duty to ensure that his land is reasonably safe for the purposes for which a person is invited or permitted to be there.

The children had not been 'invited' on to the land but there was evidence that children frequently went on to the land and that the defendants had done nothing to keep them off and they were therefore regarded as licensees, i.e., they had a limited right to be there.

On the facts, however, it was considered imprudent for a parent to have allowed two small children to go alone on to the land or, at least, a prudent parent would have satisfied himself that the place held no dangers for the children. To an adult, the danger was obvious (the plaintiff's sister managed to avoid it by walking round the end of the trench).

The defendants were entitled to assume that parents would exercise such supervision and therefore, although the plaintiff was a licensee, the defendants were not in breach of their duty to him.

PINNEL'S CASE

(1602) 5 Co Rep 117a

Notes

THE FACTS Pinnel sued Cole because Cole had failed to repay a debt of £8 10s (now £8 50p) on the agreed date, 11 November 1600. Cole's defence was that he had, at Pinnel's request, paid the sum of £5 2s 6d (now £5 12½p) on 1 October 1600 and that Pinnel had accepted this early and lesser payment in settlement of the debt.

THE DECISION It was held that due to a technical fault in the defence by Cole (a failure to plead that the lesser sum was tendered in full settlement) the claim by Pinnel would be upheld.

The common law on the repayment of debt was laid down as follows:

(a) Payment of a lesser sum on the due date cannot be any satisfaction for the whole of the debt. So a creditor who accepts part payment on the due date may still sue for the balance of the debt.

(b) Payment of a lesser sum before the due date at the request of the creditor is good consideration for the creditor's promise to forgo the balance of the debt.

(c) Payment of a lesser sum on the due date either in a different place or accompanied by an object of any value if at the request of the creditor, is good consideration for the creditor's promise to forgo the balance of the debt.

COMMENTARY These common-law rules have remained almost unchanged for nearly 400 years.

If A owes B £100 repayable on 1 January and *if* B is willing to accept say, £10 plus a pencil, the value of the pencil is good consideration to support a promise by B not to claim the balance of £90 still owing by A. It may be rather difficult to find any creditor who will agree to such an arrangement, however good in law.

Notes

PLANCHÉ v COLBURN

(1831) 8 Bing 14

THE FACTS The plaintiff had agreed to write a book for the defendants, for which he was to be paid £100. He had written part of the book when the defendants abandoned publication.

The plaintiff sued for his fee.

THE DECISION The plaintiff was entitled to half the fee on a *quantum meruit* basis.

COMMENTARY The Latin expression *quantum meruit* means 'as much as he has earned' or 'as much as he deserves'. It is an alternative remedy available in situations where the law is prepared to compel the defendant not to disappoint the plaintiff of the 'fruits of his labour'. Since the plaintiff had laboured to complete half the book, he was entitled to half the fee.

Quantum meruit is available:

(a) for work done under a contract discharged by the defendant's breach (in *Planché* v *Colburn* the defendant abandoned the publication in which the plaintiff's work was to be published);

(b) for work done under a contract which subsequenty turns out to be void. (In *Craven Ellis* v *Canons Ltd* the plaintiff was appointed managing director of a company under a contract which was not binding. He did some work for the company and the court awarded him a reasonable remuneration on a *quantum meruit* basis for the work he had done.)

RAFFLES v WICHELHAUS

(1864) 159 ER 375

Notes

THE FACTS Wichelhaus contracted with Raffles for the supply of 125 bales of cotton, the agreed price to be paid on the arrival of the cotton in the UK on a ship, the *Peerless*, from Bombay.

When the cotton arrived in the UK on board a ship *Peerless* which had sailed from Bombay in December, Wichelhaus refused either to accept the cotton or to pay the agreed price.

Raffles sued for a breach of the contract.

In reply Wichelhaus stated that he had agreed to accept and pay for cotton to be shiped from Bombay on a ship *Peerless* sailing from that port in October and had the cotton arrived in the UK as he anticipated, he would have accepted the goods and paid the agreed price.

It transpired that Raffles had no cotton shipped on the *Peerless* sailing from Bombay in October.

THE DECISION There was nothing in the contract to indicate which ship called *Peerless* was to be the agreed means of transporting the cotton. As there were two ships called *Peerless* sailing from Bombay there was a latent ambiguity in the contract.

If Raffles had in mind the use of the *Peerless* sailing from Bombay in *December* and Wichelhaus had in mind the use of another ship also called *Peerless* sailing from Bombay in *October*, there was no *consensus ad idem* (no real agreement) between the parties and consequently no binding contract.

COMMENTARY This case illustrates one of the types of operative mistake, that is, a mistake which can render a contract void or voidable. Both parties made different mistakes, known as non-identical mistakes, resulting in them being at cross purposes. This case is a leading example of a bilateral mutual mistake, mutual because both the parties made *different mistakes*.

Notes

RAMSGATE VICTORIA HOTEL CO. v MONTEFIORE

(1866) LR 1 Ex 109

THE FACTS The defendant had offered to buy shares in the plaintiff company in June. The plaintiffs tried to accept this offer in November, by which time the defendant no longer wanted them.

The plaintiffs sued for the purchase price of the shares.

THE DECISION The six-month delay between the offer in June and the 'acceptance' in November was unreasonable and so the offer had 'lapsed', i.e., it could no longer be accepted and the defendant was not liable for the price of the shares.

COMMENTARY An offer lapses (i.e., comes to an end/terminates) if it is not accepted within a 'reasonable time'. What is reasonable depends on the circumstances but it is evident that where the contract concerns something that fluctuates in price, e.g., shares, or something which may deteriorate, e.g., fresh food, the time available for acceptance is shorter than for other more durable articles.

Note: An offer comes to an end or terminates on the happening of any of the following events:

(a) if not accepted within a reasonable time (as above);
(b) if the offeror or offeree dies before acceptance;
((a) and (b) are known as lapse of offer)
(c) when revoked/withdrawn before acceptance;
(d) when rejected;
(e) when a counter-offer is made (see *Hyde* v *Wrench*, p. 62).

R v ALLEN

[1985] 2 All ER 641

Notes

THE FACTS Mr Allen was visiting London on business and booked accommodation in a large hotel for 10 days, subsequently extending his stay to 26 days, after which he left the hotel without removing his personal property or paying the hotel bill for £1,286.94. Two days after leaving Mr Allen telephoned the hotel to say that he was in financial difficulties due to delay in some business transactions but that he would collect his personal property and deposit his Australian passport as security for the unpaid hotel bill.

On his return to the hotel Mr Allen was arrested and charged with the offence under section 3(1) of the Theft Act 1978, which provides:

> A person who, knowing that payment on the spot . . . is required or expected from him, dishonestly makes off without having paid as required or expected and with intent to avoid payment of the amount due shall be guilty of an offence.

A jury convicted Mr Allen who appealed to the Court of Appeal. The Appeal Court quashed the conviction on the grounds that the offence was committed only if there was an intention never to pay.

The prosecution appealed to the House of Lords.

THE DECISION The House of Lords affirmed the decision of the Court of Appeal, holding that section 3(1) of the Theft Act 1978 was to be interpreted to mean that the making off offence was to apply only if the person making off had an intention to evade payment altogether.

COMMENTARY This decision reflected the advice of the Criminal Law Revision Committee (13th Report, 1977 Cmnd 6733), that the making off offence should apply only if there was an intention never to pay.

It seems therefore that no criminal liability attaches to a person who takes goods or benefits from services and declines to pay for them on the spot so long as it is made clear that payment will be made at a later date. This puts the provider of the goods or services into the position of having to extend credit whether he wants to or not.

R v BOWSHER
[1973] RTR 202

THE FACTS On 26 July 1970 Bowsher committed two separate sets of traffic offences.

Bowsher was convicted of the first set of offences on 19 November 1970 and was disqualified from holding a driving licence for 6 months (until 19 May 1971).

On 2 February 1971 Bowsher was convicted of the second set of offences in a different court and disqualified from holding a driving licence for 6 months (until 2 August 1971).

On 2 August 1971 the licensing authority returned Bowsher's driving licence to him and he started driving again, believing that his disqualification had expired. Whilst driving on 28 October 1971 Bowsher was stopped and required to produce his licence.

Bowsher was subsequently charged and convicted of driving on 28 October 1971 whilst disqualified, on the basis that 2 × 6 months disqualifications from 19 November 1970 did not expire until 19 November 1971.

Bowsher appealed to the Court of Appeal.

THE DECISION The Court of Appeal held that the conviction for driving on 28 October 1971 whilst disqualified was correct.

The fact that the licensing authority did not correctly apply the provisions of the Road Traffic (Disqualification) Act 1970, by returning the licence on 2 August 1971 instead of on 19 November 1971, provided Bowsher with no defence. Likewise an honest belief by Bowsher that he could resume driving was no defence.

COMMENTARY This case demonstrates that some criminal offences, including most motoring offences, carry strict or absolute liability. In other words, no excuse can be offered for committing the offence. The effect is sometimes to impose criminal liablity on blameless persons, the justification being that the harm that the particular law seeks to prevent could be serious enough to warrant this. If anybody could drive a vehicle, many persons might be harmed.

R v BYRNE

[1960] 3 All ER 1

Notes

THE FACTS Byrne strangled a young woman and then sexually mutilated her body. Byrne admitted the crime and was convicted of murder and sentenced to life imprisonment.

Byrne appealed on the grounds that all the medical evidence called at the trial indicated that he was a sexual psychopath, which is an abnormality of the mind which results in uncontrollable, violent, perverted sexual desires, and that he killed as a result of the abnormality of his mind. Consequently Byrne was entitled to rely on the defence of diminished responsibility, so could not be guilty of murder, only manslaughter.

THE DECISION Byrne was entitled to the defence of diminished responsibility, so the conviction for murder would be quashed and a conviction for manslaughter substituted. The sentence of life imprisonment would not be disturbed.

COMMENTARY The defence of diminished responsibility, introduced in the Homicide Act 1957, is intended to deal with situations where the defendant is not normal but not yet insane in the strict legal sense under the 'M'Naghten Rules', which were formulated to decide insanity following the case of Daniel M'Naghten: in 1843 M'Naghten killed Edward Drummond, secretary to Sir Robert Peel, while suffering from insane delusions of being persecuted by Sir Robert Peel.

The defence of diminished responsibility provides that:

> A person who kills is not guilty of murder if he/she was suffering from such abnormality of the mind (from any cause) as substantially impaired his/her mental responsibility for the act.

R v CHURCH

[1965] 2 All ER 72

THE FACTS Church took a woman into the rear of his van for sexual purposes but was unable to perform the sexual act. After the woman had reproached Church there was a fight in which the woman was knocked out. Church tried for about 30 minutes to revive the woman but was unable to do so. He then dragged the woman out of his van and put her body in a nearby river, where the woman drowned.

Church was convicted of manslaughter and appealed against the conviction.

THE DECISION The Court of Appeal held that Church had been properly convicted of gross negligence manslaughter.

COMMENTARY A clearer case of gross negligence causing death might be hard to find. The trial judge directed the jury: '. . . if not knowing whether the woman was dead, or not, and not having taken the trouble to find out whether she was dead, or not, he throws her body into the river, you can conclude that this was a negligent act done utterly recklessly . . .'.

R v COLLINS

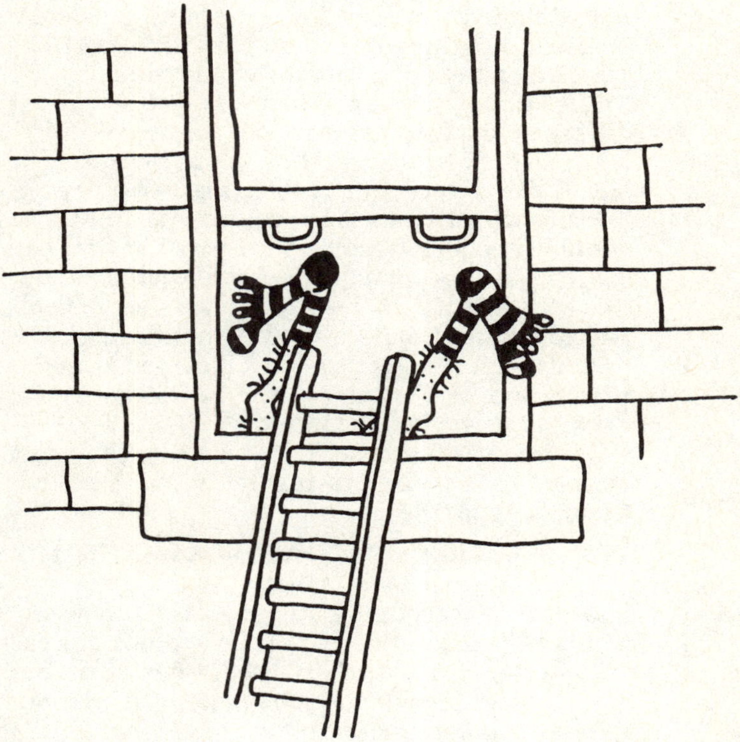

'took off all his clothes except his socks and went back up the ladder'

Notes

R v COLLINS

[1972] 2 All ER 1105

THE FACTS Collins was a painter working on a housing estate and he noticed that there was a very attractive young woman living in one of the houses. Collins went to the trouble to find out which was the young woman's bedroom window and one night in July 1971 he put a ladder up to this window, which was wide open, then climbed up the ladder and saw through the window that the young woman was asleep, naked on her bed. Collins then went down the ladder, took off all his clothes except his socks, went back up the ladder and sat perched on the outside of the window sill.

The young woman awoke to see a naked male crouched outside her window in the moonlight and jumped to the conclusion that her boyfriend (with whom she was on very intimate terms) was paying her a nocturnal visit. She sat up and Collins came through the window and joined her on the bed. After they had made love the young woman realised that there was something different about her 'boyfriend', so she turned on the bedside light and discovered her mistake. She slapped Collin's face, who replied, 'Give me a good time tonight', whereupon she went to the bathroom and Collins departed down the ladder.

Collins was convicted of burglary (entering as a trespasser intending to rape). Collins appealed to the Court of Appeal.

THE DECISION The Court of Appeal held that the conviction must be quashed. On the evidence Collins had not entered the bedroom as a trespasser, as the young lady had indicated that he was not unwelcome.

As far as could be ascertained, Collins had remained crouched on the window sill outside the window before the young woman woke up, save for one small part of him which was slightly ahead so entering the bedroom. An entry by a trespasser must be a substantial one and the part of Collins that might have entered before the young woman woke up was not substantial.

COMMENTARY As Edmund Davies LJ said: 'Were the facts put into a novel or portrayed on the stage they would be regarded as so improbable as to be unworthy of serious consideration and as verging at times on farce.'

R v DELLER

Notes

(1952) 36 Cr App Rep 184

THE FACTS Deller traded in his Standard motor car for another car, saying that there was no money owing on it and that he was free to sell the car. In fact Deller had previously signed documents which purported to effect the sale of the Standard car to another dealer and at the same time to hire the car back from a finance company. Unknown to Deller this sale and hire back of the Standard car was not effective in law as the documents were defective, so Deller merely *thought* he was falsely pretending that the car was his property when trading it in for another car.

Deller was convicted of falsely pretending to be the owner of the Standard car and he appealed on the grounds that he had, in fact, made no false pretence about the ownership of the car — the previous sale being void meant that Deller was, in truth, the owner of the Standard car at the time of its trade in.

THE DECISION The Court of Appeal held that the conviction must be quashed, as in fact Deller had made no false pretence, having, as one appeal judge put it, 'quite accidentally, and strange as it may sound, dishonestly told the truth'.

COMMENTARY The unusual facts of this case illustrate that all crimes, not merely false pretences, must have a wrongful act (an *actus reus*) and that a 'guilty mind' (a *mens rea*) is not on its own sufficient for a crime to exist.

Notes

R v DUDLEY AND STEPHENS

(1884) 14 QBD 273

THE FACTS Four people had been shipwrecked in an open boat a thousand miles from land. They were Captain Dudley, seamen Stephens and Brooks and cabin boy Richard Parker.

After 18 days adrift the Captain convinced Stephens that one of them ought to be sacrificed to save the others, and that the obvious candidate was Richard Parker. He was an orphan, had no wife or family and was already on the brink of death. One day later, Dudley and Stephens killed the cabin boy. Brooks wanted no part in the killing.

All three men survived for three more days by feeding on the boy's body. On the fourth day they were rescued in a very weak condition by a German ship. They were landed at Falmouth in Cornwall. Dudley, Stephens and Brooks went straight to the authorities and explained the reasons for the death of the boy.

THE DECISION The accused were convicted of murder after the jury had returned a special verdict finding that the men would probably have died within the four days had they not fed on the boy's body, that the boy would probably have died before them and that, at the time of the killing, there was no appreciable chance of saving life, except by killing one of the others to eat.

COMMENTARY The defence of 'necessity' was raised and rejected. The case highlights the fact that there is no general defence of necessity — except in cases of self-defence or prevention of violent crimes.

Notes: The sentence was commuted to six months' imprisonment.

R v HALLIDAY

[1886-90] All ER Rep 1028

Notes

THE FACTS Halliday, who had a reputation for domestic violence, arrived home very drunk and told his wife and daughter to go to bed. Halliday then called out to ask if they had obeyed him and on learning that this was not the case he staggered towards the bedroom shouting threats to his wife.

Mrs Halliday ran to the bedroom window to climb out but was held by her daughter on the window sill, both women being very frightened. Halliday entered the bedroom and said to his daughter, 'Let the bugger go', whereupon the daughter did so and Mrs Halliday fell from the window and broke her leg.

Halliday was convicted of causing his wife grievous bodily harm but appealed.

THE DECISION The Court of Crown Cases Reserved (now the Court of Appeal) held that if a person creates in another person's mind an immediate sense of danger which causes that person to try and escape, then if injury results from the escape attempt, the person who created such a state of mind is liable for the resulting injuries.

The conviction was upheld.

COMMENTARY This case affirms that it is possible to cause serious harm to another without any physical contact, merely by inducing a fear which results in self-inflicted harm.

Notes

R v LLOYD, BHUEE AND ALI

[1985] 2 All ER 661

THE FACTS Lloyd was the projectionist at an Odeon cinema and Bhuee and Ali were producers of 'pirate' video tapes of feature films and had high speed copying equipment to transfer cine film to master video tape from which 'pirate' copies could be produced. Between showings of feature films in the cinema Lloyd would take the reels of cine film to Bhuee and Ali for copying and all three were caught while making a copy of *The Missionary*.

All three were charged with theft and convicted by a jury.

Appeals were made on the basis that the statutory definition of theft requires an intention to permanently deprive the owner of the property and that the borrowing of the films did not come within the type of borrowing defined by statute as amounting to theft.

THE DECISION It was held by the Court of Appeal that:

(a) There was no theft of the cine film.
(b) The borrowing of the cine films did not constitute theft because the statute required that for a borrowing to amount to theft the 'goodness, virtue or capital value' of the borrowed article must be reduced by that borrowing. The cine films were still able to be shown to paying audiences.

The convictions for theft were quashed; the only offence was a breach of the law of copyright.

COMMENTARY This case illustrates the problem of deciding just when the borrowing of an article turns into the theft of that article. The relevant law is contained in section 6 of the Theft Act 1968, and has been said to 'sprout obscurity at every phrase'.

It appears that only borrowings that cause direct loss to the owner of the borrowed article can constitute theft. For example, a borrowed season ticket which is returned to the owner the day before it expires would cause loss to the owner, and so would amount to the theft of that season ticket.

R v MILLER
[1983] 1 All ER 978

Notes

THE FACTS Miller was sleeping in an unoccupied furnished house without the consent of the owner. One night Miller fell asleep while smoking and woke up to find that the bedding was on fire. Miller then went into another bedroom and went back to sleep, only to be awakened again by the fire brigade. When asked what had happened, Miller replied, 'I hadn't got anything to put the fire out with, so I just left it'.

Miller was charged with arson (causing damage by fire) under the Criminal Damage Act 1971, which provides:

> A person who without lawful excuse destroys or damages any property belonging to another intending to destroy or damage any such property or being reckless as to whether any such property would be destroyed or damaged shall be guilty of an offence . . .

Miller was convicted by a jury and on appeal the Court of Appeal upheld the conviction. Miller further appealed to the House of Lords.

THE DECISION It was held by the House of Lords that a person who, on becoming aware of a danger he has created, either:

(a) consciously takes the risk of further harm; *or*
(b) gives no thought to there being any such risk if it is an obvious risk;

is reckless.

The conviction was upheld.

COMMENTARY This case involves the very difficult issue of 'recklessness' and illustrates that a *failure* to act, as opposed to a physical act (an *actus reus*) can, in some circumstances, attract criminal liability. In the House of Lords Lord Diplock expressed dislike of the term *actus reus*, as it suggests that there must be some positive act to attract criminal liability, whereas it is the conduct of the accused person that matters.

Notes

R v MORRIS

[1983] 3 WLR 697

THE FACTS Morris took goods from the shelves of a supermarket and replaced the price labels attached to the goods with other labels showing a lesser price. At the checkout Morris was asked for, and paid, the lesser price. After leaving the supermarket Morris was arrested and charged with theft, having 'dishonestly appropriated property belonging to another'.

A jury convicted Morris and he appealed to the Court of Appeal which upheld the conviction. Morris further appealed to the House of Lords.

THE DECISION It was held by the House of Lords that the statutory definition of 'appropriates' contained in section 3(1) of the Theft Act 1968, namely:

> any assumption by a person of the rights of an owner amounts to an appropriation

was to be interpreted to mean any assumption by a person of *any* of the rights of an owner. It was not necessary to assume *all* the rights of an owner.

The House of Lords also held that the concept of appropriation involved only acts amounting to either adverse interference with or usurpation of the rights of the owner. Price label switching could interfere with one of the rights of the owner, namely to decide the selling price.

The conviction was upheld.

COMMENTARY This decision partly clarifies the law applicable to price label switching in supermarkets, etc. But as Lord Roskill put it: '. . . if a shopper with some perverted sense of humour, intending only to create confusion and nothing more, . . . switches labels, I do not think that the act of label switching alone is without more an appropriation'.

R v NEDRICK

[1986] 3 All ER 1

Notes

THE FACTS Nedrick, who bore a grudge against a woman, poured paraffin through the letter-box of the woman's house and set it alight. A child died in the resulting fire and Nedrick was charged with murder. Nedrick admitted starting the fire intending merely to frighten the woman, not to kill anyone, since when he was asked why he started the fire he replied, 'Just to wake her up and frighten her.'

By a majority the jury convicted Nedrick of murder, and he was sentenced to life imprisonment. Nedrick appealed to the Court of Appeal.

THE DECISION It was held by the Court of Appeal that a person could not be guilty of murder unless either:

(a) he intended to kill or cause serious harm; *or*

(b) he appreciated that death or serious harm was an almost certain consequence of his action.

The conviction for murder was quashed and a conviction for manslaughter was substituted with a sentence of 15 years' imprisonment.

COMMENTARY This decision develops further the law regarding criminal liability for acts resulting in death which may be described as reckless acts rather than intentional acts. With reckless acts the wrongdoer may, or may not, have thought about the possible consequences of that act.

A jury in this sort of case must now be directed that they cannot find the necessary *mens rea* (guilty mind) for murder unless they are sure that the defendant appreciated that either death or serious harm from his act was a 'virtual certainty'.

Notes

R v QUICK

[1973] 3 All ER 347

THE FACTS Quick was a male nurse in a mental hospital and suffered from diabetes, for which he took prescribed amounts of the drug insulin. Quick attacked and injured a patient and was charged with an assault causing actual bodily harm.

Quick claimed that the assault took place whilst he was suffering from hypoglycaemia (a lack of sugar), a condition common to users of insulin, and that as a result of his condition he did not know what he was doing. Consequently he was entitled to the defence of 'automatism' (involuntary actions resulting from a failure of the normal link between a person's mind and his actions).

At the trial the judge ruled that Quick could only put up the defence of insanity, so Quick changed his plea to 'guilty' and then appealed against the ruling by the trial judge.

THE DECISION It was held by the Court of Appeal that the trial judge was in error to hold that Quick could only rely on the defence of insanity. Quick was entitled to have his defence of 'automatism' left to the jury to decide.

As it was therefore not certain that the jury would have convicted Quick, the conviction was quashed as unsatisfactory.

COMMENTARY The Court of Appeal had to consider if the defendant's condition at the time of the assault amounted to 'a defect of reason from disease of the mind', which is the essential requirement for establishing insanity. Clearly the defendant's mental condition was due to an external condition, namely, the taking of insulin followed by a lack of sugar, and not to a bodily disorder in the nature of a disease which disturbed the working of his mind.

It may be thought strange that a nurse would not recognise the onset of hypoglycaemia and immediately correct it by eating a lump of sugar.

R v TOLSON

(1889) 23 QBD 168

Notes

THE FACTS The defendant was deserted by her husband in 1881 and heard from reliable sources that he had been drowned while on a voyage to America. More than five years later, believing herself to be a widow, she married again. Her husband reappeared in 1887 and she was charged with bigamy.

THE DECISION She was not guilty. It was a defence to the charge to show that she had an honest and reasonable belief that her husband was dead.

COMMENTARY Mistake is a defence where it prevents the defendant from having the necessary intent (*mens rea*) which the law requires for the crime with which he is charged.

Bigamy is the crime committed by a person who, being lawfully married, goes through a form of marriage with another person during the life of the first husband or wife. The second 'marriage' is void.

Mrs Tolson's defence of mistake to the charge of bigamy was allowed because she believed in good faith and on reasonable grounds that her husband was dead — her husband had been reported drowned at sea and had been missing for more than five years. She could therefore claim that, had she known the true facts, the crime of bigamy would not have been committed.

Note: (i) An unreasonable belief would not afford a defence. If Mrs Tolson had heard a rumour in 1885 that her husband was still alive, she probably could not have pleaded mistake. (ii) Mistake of law is no excuse — *ignorantia legis haud excusat*. This reflects the premise that everyone is presumed to know the law.

R v TOLSON

'Her husband reappeared . . .'

ROBERTS v GRAY

Notes

[1913] 1 KB 520

THE FACTS The defendant, a minor, agreed to accompany the plaintiff, a professional billiard player, on a world tour, during which he would receive instruction. A dispute arose and the minor refused to go.

THE DECISION The contract was valid and binding on the minor as it was a 'beneficial contract of service'. He was therefore liable and damages were awarded to the plaintiff for breach of contract.

COMMENTARY Contracts made by minors are valid and binding if they fall into either of two categories;

(a) contracts for 'necessaries' (see *Nash* v *Inman*, p. 77);

(b) beneficial contracts of service.

This case falls within (b), which covers any situation where a minor enters into a contract involving education, training, apprenticeship, etc. provided that, taken as a whole, it is for his benefit (see *De Francesco* v *Barnum*, p. 43).

Note: In determining what constitutes a beneficial contract of service the courts are prepared to include relationships which bear the 'hallmarks' of apprenticeship, etc. In the case *Doyle* v *White City Stadium*, for instance, a contract was made between a professional boxer (a minor) and the British Boxing Board of Control, under which the minor received a licence to box and agreed to comply with the rules of the Board. These included a term that if he were disqualified the money he was to receive for the fight would be withheld. The boxer fought a contest and was disqualified. He sued for the money and was unsuccessful, since he was bound by the agreement and its terms:

(a) It was analagous to a contract of service (i.e., it resembled an apprenticeship).

(b) It was beneficial (i.e., it enabled him to learn his 'trade' and the terms of the licence protected both contestants).

ROBINSON v KILVERT

(1889) 41 Ch D 88

THE FACTS The defendant began to manufacture paper boxes in the cellar of a house. The floor above was leased to the plaintiff. The defendant used a boiler which created hot, dry air. This raised the temperature on the floor above, damaging brown paper which the plaintiff warehoused there.

The plaintiff sued in the tort of nuisance.

THE DECISION The defendant was not liable in nuisance.

The paper stored by the plaintiff was exceptionally sensitive to heat. Ordinary paper would not have been damaged by the heating process, which did not inconvenience the plaintiff's workmen.

COMMENTARY This case illustrates that an action in nuisance will not be successful if the loss arose as a result of the particular sensitivity of the plaintiff or his property, i.e., there is no redress for damage due solely to the exceptionally delicate nature of the operations carried on by an injured party.

Lord Justice Lopes commented, 'A man who carries on an exceptionally delicate trade cannot complain because it is injured by his neighbour doing something lawful on his property, if it is something which would not injure anything but an exceptionally delicate trade.'

Note: Nuisance is an interference with a person's use or enjoyment of land. A plaintiff in nuisance need not own the land; occupation is sufficient. In this case a tenant sued.

SAYERS v HARLOW URBAN DISTRICT COUNCIL

Notes

[1958] 2 All ER 342

THE FACTS The plaintiff sustained injuries after she was trapped because of a faulty lock in a toilet maintained by the defendants. She fell while attempting to climb out by standing on the toilet-roll holder.

She sued for damages in the tort of negligence.

THE DECISION The defendants were principally to blame but the plaintiff was also at fault for standing on a 'revolving object'. Her 'contributory negligence' was assessed at 25% and her damages were accordingly reduced by that amount.

COMMENTARY The Law Reform (Contributory Negligence) Act 1945 provides that where both parties are partly to blame for a loss, a claimant's damages will be reduced in proportion to the extent to which they were responsible for that loss.

Mrs Sayers was considered to be 25% to blame, so the damages she received were 25% less than she would have received had the defendants been entirely to blame.

A common application of this principle arises in the case of car accidents — a front seat passenger injured due to the negligent driving of another will have his damages reduced if he was not wearing a seat belt, as he is regarded as being contributorily negligent for his own injuries.

Note: Where the plaintiff has been put at risk by the defendant's negligence, compelling him to choose between two or more risky alternatives, he is not guilty of contributory negligence if his choice turns out to be a mistaken one, e.g., jumping from a bus in the mistaken but reasonable belief that it was about to overturn.

SAYERS v HARLOW URBAN DISTRICT COUNCIL

'She fell while attempting to climb out by standing on the toilet-roll holder'

SIMPKINS v PAYS

Notes

[1955] 3 All ER 10

THE FACTS A grandmother, granddaughter and lodger entered a newspaper fashion competition. They won a prize of £750 but the grandmother (the defendant) refused to pay and the lodger sued for his share.

THE DECISION Although this appeared to be in the nature of a domestic agreement, there was evidence of an intention to create legal relations — it was a joint enterprise and they had agreed to 'go shares'.

The plaintiff was legally entitled to his share, i.e., £250.

COMMENTARY A contract is an agreement that is intended to have legal consequences.

The general rule is that agreements of a domestic/ social type are not intended to be legally binding. In the words of Atkin LJ, 'It is necessary to remember that there are agreements between parties which do not result in contracts within the meaning of that term in our law. The ordinary example is where two parties agree to take a walk together or where there is an offer and an acceptance of hospitality. Nobody would suggest in ordinary circumstances that those agreements result in what we know as a contract, . . . even though there may be what as between other parties would constitute consideration . . . . They are not contracts because the parties did not intend that they should be attended by legal consequences'.

This does not mean that agreements of a domestic/ social nature are *never* legally binding; the 'presumption' that they are not legally binding can be 'rebutted' — as illustrated by this case. The parties were in a domestic/social relationship but the court detected an intention to create legal relations from the informal syndicate they had created.

Notes

STILK v MYRICK

(1809) 170 ER 1168

THE FACTS Stilk, a merchant seaman, signed up for a voyage from London to the Baltic ports and return. The ship's articles (the crew agreement) provided that Stilk was to be paid at the rate of £5 per month and the articles contained a term that all the members of the crew would do all they could to ensure the safe return of the ship 'under all the emergencies of the voyage'.

In the course of the voyage two crew members left the ship and the captain was unable to obtain replacement crew at the Baltic ports. The captain thereupon agreed with Stilk and the other remaining crew members that if they sailed the ship back to London short-handed, the wages of the two crew members who had left the ship would be shared out amongst them.

The owners of the ship refused to honour the agreement made by the captain, so Stilk sued for his share of the wages of the deserted crew.

THE DECISION The agreement made by the captain of the ship with Stilk and the other crew members was not binding, as Stilk and the others had not given any consideration to support the agreement.

The desertion of the two crew members at one of the Baltic ports was an 'emergency of the voyage' and under the terms of the original agreement (the articles) Stilk was under an obligation to do all in his power to ensure the safe return of the ship.

COMMENTARY This seemingly unfair decision has to be looked at in the circumstances prevailing at the time when seamen accepted very onerous conditions, including that if freight was lost on a voyage they would not get paid.

This case illustrates the principle in the law of contract that a promise cannot be enforced unless there is good consideration given in return for that promise and, legally, Stilk did nothing for the promise of extra pay, since he did no more than he had originally promised to do.

STOREY v ASHTON

Notes

(1869) LR 4 QB 476

THE FACTS The defendant employed a driver, who was on an errand when he took a detour to do a favour for a fellow employee. He negligently knocked down and injured the plaintiff who sued on the basis that the defendant was vicariously liable for the negligence of his employee.

THE DECISION The defendant was not liable as, at the time of the accident, his employee was acting outside the course of his employment.

COMMENTARY The expression 'vicarious liability' refers to the situation where one person is liable for the wrongdoing of another. It can arise in a number of situations, e.g., parent and child, but it most commonly occurs in the employer/employee and the employer/independent contractor relationships.

The justification for imposing liability on an employer is that it:

(a) stops him hiring an employee to commit a tort;
(b) encourages him to maintain a safe system of work;
(c) is generally the case that he is in a better financial position to compensate the injured party.

This case illustrates that an employer is not vicariously liable for the torts of an employee committed outside 'the course of his employment' or who is on 'a frolic of his own'. Had the detour been slight or unavoidable, the employer would have been liable.

Note: The employer *and* employee are liable and may be sued 'jointly and severally'. This means they are individually liable and collectively liable, so the plaintiff can either sue one or the other or both. Usually only the employer is sued, on the basis that he is more likely to be able to pay the damages. If the employer is sued he may recover some or all of the loss from the employee.

SWEET v PARSLEY

[1969] 1 All ER 347

THE FACTS Miss Sweet owned a farmhouse near Oxford but did not reside there, letting all the rooms except one to students. Miss Sweet used the room she retained during her occasional visits to collect the rents and check over her property.

The police found some of the students smoking cannabis in the farmhouse and Miss Sweet was convicted by the magistrates' court of an offence under section 5(b) of the Dangerous Drugs Act 1965, which provided:

> [If a person] is concerned in the management of any premises used for any such purpose as aforesaid, he shall be guilty of an offence against this Act.

The aforesaid purpose included the smoking of cannabis.

The magistrates found that Miss Sweet had no knowledge whatever that the farmhouse was being used for such a purpose and she appealed, by case stated, to the Divisional Court, who upheld the conviction.

Miss Sweet further appealed to the House of Lords.

THE DECISION It was held by the House of Lords that in the absence of express words in the statute Parliament could not have intended the offence in section 5(b) to be one of absolute (strict) liability, thus the offence required a *mens rea* (mental element, literally a guilty mind). Since Miss Sweet had no *mens rea*, as she had no knowledge of the offence, the conviction was quashed.

COMMENTARY This case illustrates the application of the presumption that if a statute is silent about *mens rea*, absolute liability for a criminal offence cannot be imposed. As Lord Reid put it: '. . . there has for centuries been a presumption that Parliament did not intend to make criminals of persons who were in no way blameworthy in what they did. That means that, whenever a section is silent as to *mens rea*, there is a presumption that, in order to give effect to the will of Parliament, we must read in words appropriate to require *mens rea*.'

TAYLOR v CALDWELL

(1863) 122 ER 309

Notes

THE FACTS In May 1861 Taylor contracted with Caldwell for the hire of the Surrey Gardens and Music Hall on four days in the following June, July and August at a rent of £100 per day, for the purpose of a series of concerts. Between the date of the contract and the date of the first hiring the Music Hall was destroyed by an accidental fire, making the concert performances impossible.

Taylor, the hirer of the Music Hall, claimed compensation for the loss he had sustained due to Caldwell's inability to provide the Music Hall in accordance with the hire contract. The terms of the hire contract made no provision for liability in the event of the premises being destroyed before the hire dates.

THE DECISION The Queen's Bench Court held that looking at the contract of hire as a whole the parties contracted on the basis of the continued existence of the Music Hall at the time when the concerts were to be given; since its existence was something essential to the contract this became an implied term of the hire contract.

As the Music Hall ceased to exist without fault of either party both parties were to be excused from carrying out their promises. Thus Taylor was not liable for the agreed rent and Caldwell was not liable for failing to provide the Music Hall.

COMMENTARY This case on the frustration of a contract illustrates how unsatisfactory the common law was in relation to contracts that become impossible to perform (subsequent impossibility of performance) because of the principle that losses 'lay where they fell'.

Such situations are now covered by the Law Reform (Frustrated Contracts) Act 1943, which goes some way to remove the injustice of the common law.

However, consequential losses are not protected by the statute and so are often insured against.

Notes

THOMAS v THOMAS

(1842) 114 ER 330

THE FACTS In his will Mr Thomas made no provision for his wife but shortly before his death he expressed the wish that Mrs Thomas should continue to reside in his house for either the rest of her life or until such time as she remarried. After Mr Thomas died his executors entered into a written agreement with Mrs Thomas to convey the property to her for life providing that she remained a widow and paid the sum of £1 per year towards the ground rent on the property. Later the executors refused to convey the property to Mrs Thomas.

At first instance Mrs Thomas was awarded £100 damages against the executors, who appealed.

THE DECISION The sum of £1 per year to be paid by Mrs Thomas for the house might not be adequate consideration having regard to commercial letting values but it was sufficient consideration in law to support the agreement between the executors and Mrs Thomas.

COMMENTARY This case illustrates the principle in the law of contract that good consideration need not be adequate so long as it is sufficient in law.

It should be borne in mind that at the time of this case (1842) a married woman could not own money or property, etc., in her own name and that she was not protected by law should her husband die and leave her unprovided for.

VICTORIA LAUNDRY (WINDSOR) LTD v NEWMAN INDUSTRIES LTD

Notes

[1949] 1 All ER 997

THE FACTS The Victoria Laundry was unable to meet the demand for laundry services and could not take on large government dyeing contracts due to insufficient steam, so they sought a larger steam boiler. Newman Industries had a surplus steam boiler that was suitable, so they contracted to sell this boiler to Victoria Laundry, also undertaking to dismantle and to deliver the boiler on 5 June 1946.

Due to damage during dismantling the boiler was delivered 20 weeks late and Victoria Laundry sued for breach of contract claiming compensation for:

(a) loss of profits from the laundry work they could not accept for the 20 weeks;
(b) loss of profits from the government dyeing contracts they could not accept for the 20 weeks.

At first instance the Laundry was awarded only a small amount of damages, so they appealed.

THE DECISION It was held by the Court of Appeal that the principle laid down in *Hadley* v *Baxendale* (p. 54) was to be applied, namely that the party in breach of contract is to be held liable only for the losses that a reasonable person could foresee as arising naturally, i.e., 'according to the ordinary course of things'. Losses arising otherwise are not the liability of the party at fault unless that party has special advance knowledge of the circumstances that would give rise to such losses. In the words of Asquith LJ, 'for a loss to be recoverable it must be "on the cards" that such a loss would occur in the light of the knowledge of the party in breach of the contract'.

Newman Industries were liable for the loss of 20 weeks' laundry profits, but as they had no prior knowledge of the special dyeing contracts lost there was no liability for such losses.

COMMENTARY The 'rules' in *Hadley* v *Baxendale* put a limitation on the principle that the award of money damages is to put, as far as is practicable, the injured party to the contract into the position he would have been in had the contract been performed.

Notes

THE 'WAGON MOUND'; OVERSEAS TANKSHIP (UK) LTD v MORTS DOCK & ENGINEERING CO.

[1961] 1 All ER 404

THE FACTS A ship, the *Wagon Mound*, operated by Overseas Tankship (UK) was taking on fuel oil in Sydney harbour, when, due to the negligence of the crew, a large amount of oil was spilt into the harbour, where it drifted to a ship repair wharf owned by Morts Dock & Engineering Co. The fuel oil was set on fire by sparks from welding work in a ship under repair at the wharf, the resulting fire destroying the wharf. The New South Wales courts held the shipowners to be liable in negligence for the fire damage to the wharf, so they appealed to the Queen (at that time, the means of final appeal for legal disputes in New South Wales). The Queen referred the case to the Judicial Committee of the Privy Council, comprised of five Lords of Appeal in Ordinary, or 'Law Lords'.

THE DECISION The Judicial Committee held that as the fire damage to the repair wharf was not a reasonably foreseeable consequence of the negligence by the crew of the *Wagon Mound*, the shipowners were not liable and the decision of the New South Wales courts be reversed.

COMMENTARY This leading case establishes that the test of liability in negligence is based, *inter alia*, on the reasonable foreseeability of the damage happening as a result of the negligent act. As the then Lord Chancellor (Viscount Simmonds) put it: 'After the event even a fool is wise. But it is not the hindsight of a fool, it is the foresight of the reasonable man which alone determines responsibility.'

Students who wonder if oil on water can be expected to be set on fire easily should bear in mind that large amounts of oil leaked from the wreck of the *Torrey Canyon* at Land's End in 1967 could not be set on fire despite repeated attempts by the Royal Air Force.

WARNER BROS PICTURES v NELSON

Notes

[1937] 1 KB 209

THE FACTS The defendant, a film actress better known as Bette Davis, agreed to act exclusively for the plaintiff film company for a year and for no one else. During the year she contracted to act for another company.

THE DECISION The court granted an injunction to the plaintiff restraining the defendant from carrying out the contract with the other company.

COMMENTARY An injunction is an order of the court restraining a person from doing some act. It is an equitable remedy, i.e., a method of settling disputes which derives from that branch of law known as 'Equity'. The rules of Equity were developed in the former Court of Chancery and are still applicable today as 'a gloss on the common law'. They are based on what is equitable or fair; it follows that an injunction will only be granted where it is fair to do so having regard to all the circumstances of the case.

It will not be granted in a contract for personal services if its result would be to compel an employee to work for a particular employer or otherwise be redundant, e.g., if A agrees to give the whole of his time to the service of B and not to serve anybody else in any capacity whatever.

It will be granted to enforce a negative stipulation in a contract where damages would not be an adequate remedy. This case illustrates the point. The actress was not faced with the alternative of starvation or working for Warner Bros, since she had many other opportunities of earning a living.

Damages would not have been an adequate remedy, as it was the 'star quality' of this particular actress that Warner Bros required.

Notes

WELCH v CHEESMAN

(1974) 229 EG 99

THE FACTS The plaintiff transferred ownership of her house (conveyed it) to the defendant for £300. She had lived with him for many years but only conveyed the house because he had threatened her with violence. The defendant died and the plaintiff asked to have the contract set aside. The house was worth about £3,000.

THE DECISION The plaintiff was entitled to avoid the contract, which was entered into under duress.

COMMENTARY Duress occurs when a contract is entered into as a result of:

(a) actual or threatened physical violence or imprisonment;
(b) threatened criminal proceedings.

The person threatened need not be the actual contracting party, but may be the husband or wife or near relative of the party.

A contract entered into under duress is voidable at the option of the party threatened, because consent to the making of the contract is not freely given.

When a contract is voidable it means that one party has a choice — he can either treat the contract as valid and binding or he can treat it as void. His option can be exercised without reference to the other party but in cases where property has changed hands — like the house in the above case — the court is called upon to 'set aside' the contract so that the property is restored to its original owner (Mrs Welch).

USING CASES IN AN EXAMINATION

At the end of a GCSE Law course the student will have amassed details of a number of decided cases and may be wondering how to recall the case details under examination conditions. For most students there is no easy answer to the problem of recall; case details must be re-read as often as necessary. Self-testing is easily achieved by using the index to select cases at random to test recall.

But knowing a case is one thing; *knowing how to use it* is another. GCSE problem questions may or may not indicate the area of law involved and sudents must be prepared, if necessary, to identify the area of law with which the problem is concerned as a vital first step in preparing an answer.

EXAMPLES OF PROBLEM QUESTIONS

Where the area of law involved is NOT stated in the question

> John sees a 'designer sweater' in a shop window with a price tag attached. The price tag reads 'SPECIAL OFFER—ONE ONLY @ £2.50'. Thinking he has found a bargain, John enters the shop and says he will buy the sweater marked at £2.50 in the window. The assistant, realising there has been an error, says that the sweater has been incorrectly priced and the correct price is £12.50.
>
> Advise John if he is legally entitled to the sweater at the marked price of £2.50.

This is a typical problem question on the law of contract, more specifically that part of contract law dealing with the formation of a contract known as 'invitation to treat'.

Two cases are applicable to this problem situation: *Fisher* v *Bell* (p. 51) and *Pharmaceutical Society of Great Britain* v *Boots Cash Chemists (Southern) Ltd* (p. 86). A reading of these cases will confirm the point at issue, namely that the display of goods in a shop, whether priced or not, is an invitation to treat and not an offer to sell; which means the prospective purchaser is invited to offer to buy the goods.

Students should not be misled by the fact that the price tag refers to it being a 'special *offer*'. This is a red herring — a trap to confuse the student with insufficient knowledge.

So, John is not accepting an offer, merely responding to an invitation to treat by making an offer to buy the sweater for £2.50.

The assistant does not have to accept this offer and in this case (realising there has been an error) does not do so. Instead the assistant makes a new offer — John can have the sweater if he is prepared to accept the new offer price of £12.50. John can decline this new offer but cannot insist on having the sweater at £2.50.

Where the area of law involved IS stated in the question

> Fred has his own road transport business and one day, while driving his lorry well within the speed limit, Fred knocks down and injures Bill, an elderly pedestrian, while Bill is attempting to cross the road.
>
> Fred does not admit any liability, saying that Bill attempted to cross the road without looking to see if it was safe to do so. An independent witness of the accident says that Fred was looking at and shouting to another lorry driver at the time of the accident.
>
> Advise Bill, who wishes to claim in the tort of negligence against Fred. How, if at all, would your advice to Bill differ if in fact Bill did not look to see if it was safe to cross the road before attempting to do so.

This is a typical question on the tort of negligence and although the examiner has indicated that is the main area of law involved, it is left to the student to see that contributory negligence is also involved in the problem.

Two cases are applicable to this problem situation: *Donoghue* v *Stevenson* (p. 48) and *Sayers* v *Harlow Urban District Council* (p. 111).

In *Donoghue* v *Stevenson* the House of Lords established the principle that every person has a legal duty of care not to do anything that can be reasonably foreseen as likely to injure a 'neighbour'. This means any person who could be so affected by the act, that the doer of that act ought to have such persons in his mind.

Applying this principle:

(a) Does Fred owe a legal duty of care not to injure all other road users, including Bill?

(b) Can Bill be considered a 'neighbour' in law to Fred?

(c) Is it reasonably foreseeable that a failure by a lorry driver to keep a continuous look-out for other road users may result in injury to them?

Affirmative answers indicate that Bill has a valid claim against Fred in negligence.

But if Bill contributed to the accident and thus to his injuries by not looking to see if it was safe to attempt to cross the road, this is contributory negligence and Bill's compensation will be reduced by the amount that the judge considers Bill was to blame. This principle was applied in the case of *Sayers* v *Harlow Urban District Council* and Mrs Sayers, who had contributed to her injuries, had her compensation reduced by 25%, the amount the judge considered that Mrs Sayers was to blame.

THE OVERALL APPROACH

To sum up, armed with the correct point of law and relevant case(s) the student should unite the two in his answer as follows:

(a) Identify the area of law concerned if it is necessary to do so.
(b) Explain the legal principle(s) involved.
(c) Support the answer with *relevant* case law, e.g., 'A case which illustrates this point is v , where the facts were . . . . ., and it was held that . . . . .'.
(d) Answer the *examiner's* question. In the examples given above:

— Is John legally entitled to the sweater at the marked price of £2.50?
— Has Bill a valid claim in negligence against Fred and how is that claim affected if Bill contributed to the accident?

It is not all that uncommon for examination candidates to forget the examiner's question in the heat of the moment and produce an answer to a question they have thought up!

Finally:

(a) It is generally better to avoid using the first person — 'I think that . . .'. Remember, it is legal principles that are being quoted, not your own opinions.
(b) Always underline case names.
(c) If the details of a case can be recalled but not the name of that case, say 'In a decided case where . . .'. So long as the description of the facts/decision is recognisable the examiner will not usually deduct marks for the lack of a case name.

Notes

Notes

Notes

Notes

Notes

Notes

Notes

Notes

Notes

Notes

Notes

Notes

Notes

Notes

Notes

Notes

Notes

Notes

Notes